Trust
And Allow
The Process
Of Life,
In-Joy!

Channeled messages from Orion

translated by
Leslie Stewart

TRUST AND ALLOW THE PROCESS OF LIFE, IN-JOY!
Channeled Message from Orion

© 2013 Leslie Stewart

ISBN 978-1-891067-04-4
Library of Congress Control Number: 2013933874

For information, contact
Leslie Stewart
P.O. Box 181212
Fairfield, Ohio 45018
513-942-3009
www.theorionchannel.com
lstewart.orion@gmail.com

Book design: Barbara With
Photograph: Vickie Rogers

The author of this book does not dispense medical advice or prescribe the use
of any technique as a form of treatment for physical, emotional, or medical
problems without the advice of a physician, directly or indirectly. The intent
of the author is only to offer information of a general nature to help you in
your quest for emotional and spiritual well-being. In the event you use any of
the information in this book for yourself, which is your constitutional right, the
author and the publisher assume no responsibility for your actions.

Dedicated to all of those who hear the calling of the self within and want to nurture it with love of self, and to my parents who were my teachers to learn unconditional love, and to my brothers Steve and Scott who live unconditional love. Finally yet most importantly, my spiritual partner Ken, who has encouraged me every step of my way on this path of greater understanding of the soul self.

Most importantly, it is for all of us who continue to dream and be inspired by the joyous co-creative process of dancing with life!

ACKNOWLEDGEMENTS

It has been my honor to have in my life many special individuals who have given of their time, wisdom, and knowledge to help me bring this project to fruition.

First, I must thank Linda White for continuously asking the questions and having a fervent desire to acquire more knowledge and understanding of the true self. Linda spent hour upon hour transcribing the material and asked questions that she felt you the reader would be interested in. My love eternally.

To Rachelle Rogers, a wonderful friend and a beautiful traveler along this path, as well as my editor who could actually make sense of what was being conveyed and was able to craft the words in an understandable, readable way.

To Barbara With, who has the knowledge and creativity to shape the book and illustrations in a way that is exceptional. A special note of appreciation to Kathy Sawyer for her assistance and Vickie Rogers for her photography.

Lastly, but with foremost thanks for Orion, my spiritual teachers, as well as for other teachers, including Gordon Stonehouse and Amel and Jeff King and Teach—and for their message, which remains constant: *Be true to self!*

We all live in a physical reality that comes to life from how we choose to create based on our experiences. We must remind ourselves to be kind to others and to ourselves and to enjoy those individuals who choose to come play with us in the here and now!

In-Joy!

TABLE OF CONTENTS

FOREWORD

Why does anyone consult with a life coach, a counselor, a psychic or an astrologer? Why does anyone read a self-improvement book? Why does anyone play bingo or the lottery, go to horse races or casinos? We do these things because we are seeking hope! We seek hope because often we are less than confident that we can achieve our fervent desire for something more than we are currently experiencing, and something we believe will bring us relief or fulfillment, pleasure or joy!

Why do people go to medical doctors, faith healers, health food stores, alternative health practitioners or ingest seminars, books, classes, diets, herbs, medicine, and vitamins? The reason is to heal their disease and pain or to prevent disease and pain. We all want to be well and to be comfortable in our bodies.

Perhaps you want a new relationship. Maybe you want more money in your life for any reason at all. You may be dreaming of a more extravagant home or simply a place to call home. You may want to take a grand vacation or maybe just a day off. Regardless of the specific goal in mind, all efforts, at their core, are attempts to attain a better-feeling feeling. We are all wired to thrive, not merely survive. So we all hope for a more and more enjoyable life. However, if you have been working too hard for this, and doubting if you can attain it, I must ask, "How's that been working for you?"

Now is the time for *Trust and Allow the Process of Life, In-Joy!*, a fitting and good title for a book that soothes us as it shows us the way to achieve our desires. Within its pages, you will find the message that visceral trusting in yourself and the universe and getting out of your own way is the solution to every problem. Read and be encouraged to let go of your struggle and allow in the goodness. *Trust and Allow the Process of Life, In-Joy!* is not just one of the best titles of any book I have ever seen, but an excellent and effective affirmation.

A visceral trusting in yourself and the universe and getting out of your own way is the solution to every problem, challenge or key to attract the essence of any desire.

Trust and Allow the Process of Life, In-Joy! inspires us to nurture in ourselves a confident expectation of attaining what we desire. In its pages, Orion teaches us the natural laws that not only support our desire to feel good, but are the foundation of life on our planet and throughout the universe as well. These gentle teachers/facilitators give illustrations and insights, which catalyze our self-discovery and self-empowerment.

Orion reminds us that we are more than our physical selves and we are connected to greater parts of our multidimensional selves that have the potential to create worlds!

Orion reiterates what their colleagues teach: In the entire universe, there is only a source of well being! There is no source of darkness. There is just resisting the light. And there is no shortage of resources, just a resistance of the abundance asked for. Our fear of evil and lack come from early imprinting from ideas heard from our family, friends, community, and institutions. It takes a wee bit of effort to illuminate these past ideas and embrace and live a more promising belief system.

Leslie and I have made great strides, thanks in large part to our invitation and participation with Orion. They have assisted us in a felt understanding that we are experiencing the magnificent gifts of joyousness. By practicing our trust in these natural laws, we now know with certainty that life is always supporting us and that well-being is not the exception, but the rule — if we can simply get out of our own way. I am so happy that Orion's message is now, in print, and right here for you.

Orion explains how many of our problems are due to our belief in scarcity. This belief is a misunderstanding of huge proportion. Orion can help you clarify this misunderstanding within your own life experience. I have learned from Orion that scarcity beliefs can even cause health challenges.

Orion repeatedly reminds us to be true to self and that we have the necessary tools and guidance within us to live the life of our dreams. Remembering this can help us to rely less and less upon outer authority and more and more on our inner authority. Our society has given undue power to the doctrine of medicine, religion, and science, even if it did not feel true for us. What a relief to remember that we have sophisticated inner guidance system thanks to the fact that we are connected to an unlimited system of universal intelligence. In other words, we are living in a divine partnership with God. I had written in my book, *Beliefology*, that man has created God in man's image. Orion helps us to get beyond this limitation and utilize a conscious partnership with our greater internal Godhood. We are not ever alone—because there is no separation!

This book comes to fruition at the perfect time because more and more people are ready to see beyond this version of reality, which has literally scared many people to death!

In our shared reality, we have been taught to be fearful of most everything, even for our own safety! We have been taught to be critical of everything, to be considered smart! However, this is changing. Orion assures us that we live in a benevolent universe, that we are worthy of joyousness, and that Life is unceasingly FOR us!

A popular tenet of teachers like Orion is that you can create or attract the essence of anything you want. Back in the 1970s when I started to conduct Seth Seminars nationwide I put out to the universe that I wanted to attract a spiritual partner to translate spirit like Jane Roberts. Jane Roberts, perhaps the most popular translator, communicated the energy essence personality Seth. In the 1980s my dream came true, and I attracted Leslie and eventually Orion. When Orion appears they bring not only words of wisdom but also emits peaceful, gentleness, and so much love that it leaves you feeling a sense of hopefulness and equanimity.

Leslie and I hope that you let the words of Orion lead you to the feeling of peace that comes with trusting and the feeling of joy that comes from knowing your own power as a conscious and loving creator.

Orion guides us to an inner and outer exploration of ourselves. When we truly feel the meaning of their words, we are helped in our knowing that the true nature and power of God is within us. This is truly a divine partnership. We can utilize a conscious partnership with our great internal Godhood and live a story of deep empowerment and creativity. Hear the words on these pages and let your life unfold in abundance and joy! My expectation is that the words of our new best friends, Orion, will encourage you on your journey to *Trust and Allow the Process of Life, In-Joy!*

Thank you Orion for nudging us to allow this grace and to flow within the ease and comfort of our own being! Welcome to the joyous experience of *Trust and Allow the Process of Life!* (... and more importantly, doing it all ...) *In-Joy!*

Ken Routson
January 14, 2013
Author of *Beliefology: Raise Your Consciousness to Wealth, Health and Happiness!*, *Beliefology Workbook* and *Internal Life*

INTRODUCTION
Leslie Stewart

When I met my spiritual partner, Ken Routson, in 1981, I found that he and I shared a resonance with the progressive and provocative ideas presented in the series of Seth books channeled by Jane Roberts in the 1970s. Seth, an "energy essence personality," said that we create our reality through our thoughts, beliefs, emotions, and intent, and that the point of power is in the present moment. In *The Nature of Personal Reality*, Seth explained how we could consciously create a joyful, fulfilling life.

At the time, Ken was a student of several other non-physical teachers—the "Teaching, Healing, and Creating Entities" who communicated through Carin Waddell via automatic writing; Teach, channeled by Jeff King; and Amel, channeled by Ken's friend, Gordon Stonehouse. Ken and I together continued to learn much from these wonderful beings, and I, like Ken, felt a passion to share with others all that we were learning and how we could implement it in our lives.

Years later, in 2005, on my fifty-second birthday, a beautiful, sunny January 27th, Ken and I were on vacation at a charming inn on Coco Beach, Florida. We were reading *Ask and It Is Given*, by Jerry and Esther Hicks, channeled information about the universal law of attraction brought forth through Esther from Abraham, a collective of loving, non-physical entities. Ken and I talked about how wonderful it would be to live, like Esther and Jerry, an abundant and joyful lifestyle by following our passion to uplift and assist others in their empowerment. It was strange, but I felt that I, too, could do what Esther does—

bring forth the larger perspective and wisdom of loving, non-physical beings. This did not come from arrogance, but from a deep desire and knowing that the ability was within me, and that if I held that focus and did what was required, the experience would be mine.

From then on, I started to meditate on a regular basis. My first intent was to receive automatic writing. Two weeks after our return from Florida, things took an encouraging turn. Ken heard that his elementary school principal had died and he wanted to attend the visitation. When we got there, I chose to stay in the car. It was an unusually warm and sunny February day for Ohio, and I had the car windows down. The birds were singing, the sun buttering the seat. I always kept pen and paper with me, and I started jotting down notes about the day and about my feelings, when I suddenly felt the pen begin to move without any conscious assistance from me. I relaxed further and let the information flow.

When Ken returned to the car, he found me in tears.

"Why are you crying?" he said. "You didn't even know this man."

"They're tears of joy," I told him. "I just received my first automatic writing."

For the rest of the winter, as I practiced letting go and relaxing into it, the automatic writing continued and progressed. One of the first things I wanted to know was who these beings I was communicating with were, and if there was a name I could call them. We came to agree on Orion because of my fascination with the stars and galaxies. Even as a small child, I would gaze for hours at the heavens, mesmerized by celestial patterns, wondering what lay beyond. Orion explained that although they may be called Orion, as in the constellation Orion, they were not from any particular planet or galaxy far away, but were a collective consciousness of All That Is. They further explained, "This energy essence of Orion or Seth or Abraham or Amel needs no name, for we are all energy, just as you are all energy." They said that some referred to them and their collaboration as the Teaching, Healing, and Creating Entities.

Spring arrived, and in April of 2005, as we had done in previous years, Ken and I went to an Abraham workshop being given at the Biltmore Inn on the beautiful Biltmore Estate in Asheville, North Carolina. At these gatherings of several hundred people, only a few got chosen to come up and ask a question. Ken was one of the lucky ones, although, as we were so often taught, "luck" had nothing to do with it. Ken asked his question.

"Leslie and I would like to have what Esther and Jerry are having. Are we on the right track?"

In reference to my channeling, Abraham's response was encouraging. They said the audience was already in my "vibrational escrow," and that all I needed was to align with that desire.

Over the next two months, I joyfully continued to do just that, and on the morning of Saturday, July 2, something magical happened. Since spring, Ken and I had been sitting on our balcony overlooking the woods beyond our condominium. I meditated while he read. One morning, I was in a relaxed and focused state, when suddenly a hummingbird appeared. Never before had I seen a hummingbird around our condominium. It hovered over me, landed momentarily on my shoulder, and flew away. It was phenomenal. I closed my eyes and listened to the birds and little creatures playing in the trees. I felt my body sway and my head begin to bob slowly from side to side. Ken said this went on for about forty-five minutes. Then, for the first time, Orion spoke.

It was a brief communication, maybe five to ten minutes, choppy and not fluent. Ken told me that Orion said it would take a while for me to acclimate to the new energy, and that I should prepare to have many more encounters.

As I became more comfortable with the process, each new session required less meditation time for me to line up to the energy, and the communications—or more accurately my translations of the blocks of thought from Orion—became more fluent. As the melding of the physical and non-physical was fine-tuned, subsequent sessions became longer and more articulate.

On the following pages, Orion will speak for themselves, offering their love, wisdom, and guidance. Most of all, they want us to know this:

You have the power. You are the creator. And when you are in sync and in harmony with your own self-directed behavior—by that we mean being in touch with your True self and following your own direction, listening to your own voice within—you will find that you have all the answers you need to create whatever you desire.

In Joy,
Leslie

Note: Most of the questions presented in the Question and Answer section of each chapter were asked in intimate conversation with Orion by Ken and our dear friend Linda White. Some additional questions came from participants in larger groups or workshops.

CHAPTER 1

Orion Speaks

Although we come here with joy to share with you the natural universal laws, we must say that you have always had this knowing within every fiber of your being. We are your reminder that you can trust and allow the process of life. Because life by its very essence, nature, and purpose is always bringing you well-being, abundance, health, vitality, and joy. It is only through your fear and self-doubt that you pinch off the natural flow and awareness of the partnership between your physical self and your larger non-physical self. You may restrict and resist the natural energy flow, but you can never completely cut yourself off from the infinite and permanent non-physical you. You are a powerful, worthy, and deserving part of that eternal collective consciousness.

It is our—the teaching, creating entities—intent to assist those who are interested in reclaiming their power and becoming the conscious creators they so fervently desired to be when they chose to come into this time-space reality. Unlike what you may have been told, the Earth experience is not inferior to the non-physical aspects of All That Is. Although less permanent, and from a less conscious perspective, the physical self is a much valued, magnificent, beautiful, purposeful expression of what some may call the God self. This physical playground is literally grounded in freedom of expression and the magic of physical manifestation. All for the joy, and spiritual evolution of each individual personality, which contributes to the eternal expansion of All That Is.

You are all divine beings. You see the evidence of your connection with your inner God self everyday. Oftentimes you will receive an answer to a question you may have through a thought or a picture of something in your minds eye, and then ah-ha! There it is. The thought produced an image, an answer. On the other hand, you might get a nudge to pick up a book or turn on the television, and an answer appears. Or the person you are speaking to answers a question you have not even asked, but merely held in your mind.

How does this magic work? You come from the source of benevolence, the source of well-being, the source of the greater part of you, and yet you continue to disbelieve and wonder how this magic works. We are with you every step of the way. All you have to do is listen to that which is you, that which is the true self, the essence from which you come and which you are at all times. This being is the inner guidance we speak of. Listen to the voice within. That true authentic self of you. That which is the divine being of you. Listen to it.

We do not want anyone to follow any particular teacher, thought, religion, or book. We want everyone to think for himself or herself. Put on the jacket of life. How does it feel? Is the fit something *you* like on yourself, not because someone else says it looks good on you? More importantly, you are not putting it on for anyone or anything outside of yourself. Enjoy the fit. Discover what feels good to you, looks good to you. Enjoy the moment, the now. We want individuals to realize for themselves what feels best, not to seek anyone else's approval or disapproval, nor to look to a particular teacher, book, or religion. Nothing outside of self. To know the self always comes from within.

Make decisions from that point of power, from that inside knowing. Be an individual. Remain true to self, remain clear that you are the one making decisions for yourself. Do not allow others, or the laws of the land to be placed upon you. *You* rule your life. About that, we want to be emphatically clear.

We smile with delight when we see you have those ah-ha moments in which you find the evidence of life giving you answers to your questions. You know that is how it works. Be more aware of that evidence as it appears to you. When you trust and allow the process of life, life gives you what you are asking for. When you trust that the answer will be given to you, you will more easily go with the flow. There is nothing hard about it. It is the individual that gets in the way of self and makes life more complicated than it needs to be or is.

Be aware of your habitual emotional responses to events. Step back for just a moment, and in that quick second of time, you will have the evidence of your beliefs or your thoughts or your thinking patterns. In time, you will become more and more aware of those thinking patterns. Awareness is the first step. Change the patterns of thought if they are no longer being of use to you, change the thinking. Then new thought patterns will emerge almost instantaneously and begin to take hold.

Know that you will continue to emerge into new thought patterns as you continue to grow and think and rethink and learn and experience and enjoy the process of life. When your awareness is keen and your responses wise, you become an active participant and player in your life. The awareness will bring forth greater understanding of the soul self, the inner self, the greater self, the authentic self, the self of you. The essence of your being. We are all divine beings here to enjoy this magnificent world. Be at peace with what is. Be aware of your thought and feeling patterns and tweak them as needed. Be easy and gentle with yourselves and know that we are all in this together having a joyful time.

Questions and Answers

Question: What is your purpose for coming to Leslie? Do you have a message?

Orion: Our message is that you have the power. You are the creator, and when you are in sync and in harmony with your own self-directed behavior—by that we mean being in touch with your true self and following your own direction, listening to your own voice within—you will find that you have the answers. You have the power to create whatever it is that you choose to create.

Question: What or who is God? What is our relationship with God, and what is our purpose as human beings?

Orion: God is whatever you choose to call that energy that exists everywhere. For wherever you look, there is the god/goddess essence of All That Is. All That Is exists as universal energy. You are a part of that universal energy. You are not separate from it. What you choose to call it does not matter. The link between you and what exists is what is of the utmost importance. You are a part of this creative energy essence. It is yours. There is no separation. So in this knowing that there is no separation, you can aspire, dream, hope, wish, and fulfill ambitions. It is all yours when you align yourselves to that energy essence. When you are truly connected, truly feeling that divine energy resonating from the bottom of your toes to the top of your head, you feel exhilaration, excitement, and the joy of life.

Question: For someone who is in a tough situation in life—maybe they've just been through a divorce or bankruptcy or something really challenging—is there any advice that you could give to help them?

Orion: When you are going through challenges that have been a part of your life for a while and now have come to an explosive head, look for the new beginning that is a result of that final burst of energy, that final letting go of past beliefs, past burdens, or past feelings of inadequacy or unworthiness. We wish all of you would see it in that way, that it is indeed a new beginning.

In that new beginning, you have much to look forward to. If you have realized for yourselves that you have created the "yuck," or what is not working in your life, you can begin creating all that is grand and glorious. What you are leaving behind has been the catalyst for what you are creating now.

Question: What is the purpose of humans on earth?

Orion: To enjoy, to express yourselves, and to experience life to the fullest.

Question: But a lot of people feel limited by their circumstances in life. What are some of the ways that we can surmount those things?

Orion: Yes. It is in limiting beliefs that one places upon themselves that hardships seem to be the rule rather than the exception when you are in this place where you feel that your life is nothing but pain and sorrow. It is when you are so encapsulated in that heavily laden feeling of unworthiness and fear that you cannot move forward. When you become so paralyzed by fear, doubt, and unworthiness, we want you to realize for yourselves that you have indeed given all of your power away. It is now time for each of you to reclaim that power that has always been yours. In the reclaiming of yourself and your power, there is a feeling of hope.

When you look at life though the eyes of self-fulfillment, self-desires, retrieving what is yours and putting those pieces of self back together, you become self-directed, self-knowing, and self-reliant. Moreover, through this you begin looking forward and not over your shoulder at what happened in the past. You begin to see all the possibilities that are in front of you. For what lies in front of you is everything that you desire, everything that you choose to be a part of. Remind yourself that you are doing the best that you can at that moment, and know that with each step forward you are making progress.

Question: Many people claim to be channeling Ascended Masters. Can you comment on what that means?

Orion: It is much like individuals on your earth plane, the belief that an individual that has several letters after their name must be more intelligent then those who have nothing after their names. Therefore, if someone that has Ph.D. he must be an ascended master of life. Ascended Masters means nothing to us for there is no hierarchy and there is no "better than." You are all beings that are connected to this source energy of All That Is, and there are no masters or Ascended Masters. We are all part of the same energy stream.

CHAPTER 2

On The Road with Orion
Charlotte, North Carolina

Rosedale Jones and Grant Ehret, who we met at the Abraham workshop in Asheville in 2006, hosted the group gathering in Charlotte. As I was preparing the way for Orion to come through, Rosedale shared the following story.

"I was standing outside at my friend's house, waiting for Leslie and Ken to arrive," she said. "Now, I am a city girl, from New York, so I was taking in the sights, smells, and sounds of the country. Suddenly, I felt this thing fly by me. It looked too big to be some kind of bug, and I really didn't know what in the world it was. When I asked my friend, she said, 'Rosedale, it's a hummingbird!' I had no idea what a hummingbird looked like. I'd never seen one until that moment."

I recalled how, right before Orion spoke for the first time, a hummingbird had appeared out of nowhere and hovered over me. Now another one had appeared in an unlikely place, once again heralding Orion's arrival. Since then, whenever a hummingbird— in any form—crosses my path, I know that it's Orion dropping in.

We are pleased to be with you. We were invited down to Charlotte by Rosedale and Grant who inspired us, and we want to assist in inspiring you. We have been visiting the south through Leslie's eyes, and she is experiencing the beautiful autumn day. We hope that you are doing the same—being, living, and enjoying each moment. Cherishing and savoring the beauty that surrounds you. The beauty that is seen through the eyes of each one of you. You are each exuding your energies and aligning yourselves with the essence of All That Is. You are all here because you know that you are on this leading edge and how exciting it is to be a part of this collective energy.

Throughout the world, there appears to be much turmoil, but in reality, what exists in the essence of All That Is is peace, tranquility, hope, and love. No matter how it may seem on the surface, everything is in divine order. It is when attention is given to things like war, poverty, devastation that the energy gets skewed. But when you focus on the beauty and wonder of life, then you experience life through all of its glorious and inspiring aliveness and joy.

This is what you are all about. You are all here because you believe that you can indeed be the creator of that and much more. Because when you know that you create your life experience through your thoughts, feelings, and beliefs, whatever you place your attention upon draws to it a like vibration that manifests in this reality. When the media gives you pictures of turmoil, it's easy to allow it into your consciousness and thereby concentrate on it. We say, look instead at all the beauty, all the abundance in the world. Give your attention to all the wonder of the universe.

The messages that we, the teachers, are conveying to you is to enjoy life, to live life with the knowing that when you are fully engaged in each life-giving moment, you see the beauty. You realize that you have created it, that there is no separation between you and what exists around you. When you see flowers in the springtime make a new appearance, or you gaze upon the trees in new bloom, isn't it amazing how it all comes about naturally? Live your lives naturally. When you see the sunrise in the sky, or enjoy the wonder of a new dawn, or feel the wind through your hair, embrace it all, because it is all yours to enjoy.

Make each day grand and glorious. Life is to be filled with joy, happiness, and fulfillment. Love yourselves, because you are all divine beings. You are here in this time, this place, this reality to experience life fully. Love one another, for when you see yourselves experiencing this love, and the peace and harmony it brings, it will soon spread throughout the world.

QUESTIONS AND ANSWERS

Questioner: If for instance, you may have had critical or judgmental parents that may have tried to ridicule you about a few extra pounds and your self-esteem was low due to that, how would you address that?

Orion: Good self-esteem and self-empowerment are the most important ingredients in most human challenges. It is important for the individual to try to understand that the individuals that are critical are the ones that are lacking in self-esteem, and they are passing that on to their children. It is ironic in a way, the parents believe they are instilling something empowering when in reality they are doing just the opposite. Understanding that concept and realizing that you do indeed have the power to either believe in your own self worth or to give your power away.

Questioner: What do I do when I experience fear? Sometimes I feel I am overwrought with fear. How do I trust myself more?

Orion: We like the acronym for fear = the **false evidence appearing real** has been conjured up in your mind's eye, and if you examine it, you can find the belief that has created it. It is this examination, this dissecting and discarding process, which will show you what you are wanting. Through this process, life will let you see what you have created by default. Then, when you are ready to get rid of it, you can create a new experience and a new way of looking at the situation. Anything that you do not want can be changed as easily as it has been created. Do you see?

Questioner: So we change it from fear to love. From fear to acceptance, and from acceptance to love.

Orion: Precisely!

Questioner: How do I know if I should continue to pursue a certain service that I was led to, when little things keep getting in the way. Can I be in the wrong place or doing the wrong thing?

Orion: This service, does it make you feel passionate and alive?

Questioner: As I am doing it, yes.

Orion: And when you are not?

Questioner: I am not sure. At one moment yes and the next moment no.

Orion: And what led you to this in the first place?

Questioner: I guess the universe. It just happened when it happened, something I wish would have happened when I was young. It has opened up a new life, a spiritual one.

Orion: Does it bring you Joy?

Questioner: Yes.

Orion: And when you are in this joy-filled life, how does it feel?

Questioner: I feel connected when I do this unconditional love service. I would like to carry this into my day-to-day life, but I have trouble letting go of ego and fear.

Orion: When the ego and fear crops up, is there any particular circumstance that makes you feel this way?

Questioner: I think there are things left over from other lifetimes that evoke reactions.

Orion: When you are in the process of releasing those fears, are you fully aware of that which has occurred and why it happened?

Questioner: Through my studies, I think I have become aware, but it is still difficult to release old habits. I am confused.

Orion: Most confusion is due to resistance. As your resistance becomes less, so will your confusion. You are still holding on to old habitual emotional responses, not from other lives, but from this one. As you become more aware of your limiting beliefs and move confidently toward this path that is calling you, then you will allow the beauty, the joy, the love, and the beingness of you. You will fully allow that energy to exude from you, and you will find that resistance dissipates. Through clearing your mind and using meditation, by listening to your inner guidance, you will gradually become the beingness that will be reflected on your new path.

Questioner: I have had a goal for the last four months and haven't seen a shift or evidence of it coming. The goal means changing my job and where I have lived for the last twenty-one years, so I have lots of resistance and fear, but I really want it.

Orion: So this thing, can it be done in Charlotte? You have created it and you realize that it would require a physical move as well as an emotional move, and you are not quite ready for an emotional move? Is that not so?

Questioner: I guess I will have to think about that. I thought I was ready for it.

Orion: If you were indeed ready, it would have manifested. For when all of your energies have been aligned, and when you are focused and bring to fruition that which you are wanting, it will come to you. You are putting too much hesitation on it. Relax and enjoy the ride and it will come.

Questioner: I am trying to overcome the belief that life is hard and a struggle.

Orion: When you look at life being hard and a struggle, you will see that life does indeed give you a hard time. Your life's experiences are merely a reflection of your beliefs. When you look at life the way it was meant to be—easy, joy-filled, and delightful—life will respond in that way. When you relax into the ease and comfort of your own being, knowing that you are the creator of your reality, you will be in the joy of life.

When you compare yourself to others saying, "Look what they have," and asking, "Why am I not getting it?" you are in resistance and not allowing the beautiful, abundant, creative life force that exudes through you. When you feel this power then you will become aware that you are not separate from All That Is, only shut off because of conditioning and erroneous beliefs. All you have to do is turn on the switch.

Questioner: Speaking of being connected. Periodically I feel energy surge through various parts of my body. What is happening?

Orion: Ken likes to use this example: When you have the garage door remote in your hand and press the button the door goes up. The remote is sending and transmitting a signal to the receiver, and lo and behold, the door opens. You send and receive signals in the same way constantly. You are all energy vibrational beings.

Questioner: I, like many women, have given my power away and even had the snot beat out of me when I tried to assert myself. As I am getting older, I am beginning to take that power back. Sometimes, however, I perceive that some people are trying to control me, and when I assert myself, it seems to happen more, perhaps because I am resisting. Can you help me with this?

Orion: Control issues are prominent in many lives both male and female, and I believe there are many others in the room that can relate to what you are saying. The position of being controlled is indeed the feelings of not being good enough, and you have attracted those in your life who want to control because of your vibrations of vulnerability. The good thing is you are aware and realizing this, and therefore you can correct it. Realize and affirm that you are enough. That you are a worthy, deserving, and connected being. You have and are the power, and no one can take that from you unless you do not believe you have this power. Know that you are connected to All That Is, and All that Is is a part of you. How can you not feel powerful? You can feel and resonate with that power when you are out with nature and vibrating with the aliveness of the trees, plants, and animals. You know they are all connected to you.

Questioner: My power cannot leave me unless I give it away. So I guess I need to feel my own power more often so I won't give it away. Then I will not have to worry about power struggles.

Orion: The only struggle there ever truly is, is with self.

CHAPTER 3

Natural Universal Laws

The following truths are the universal guiding principles applicable to consciousness both physical and non-physical, to every being, every fiber, and every particle of All That Is.

1. God is All That Is—an infinite energy essence that eternally expresses itself throughout the conscious universe with inexhaustible power and boundless, unconditional love. There is no place where God is not. Humans are not separate from God and are powerful co-creators when they live from the knowing of the true self.

Although your overall entity is difficult to explain, it is important to realize that your total self is the integration of your physical mind and body in cooperative, harmonious concert with your greater, non-physical over soul or inner self. This synergistic alliance is creating, experiencing, and expressing in the quest for joy and fulfillment. Once humans realize the scope and power of their collective selves, they can begin to viscerally perceive a glimpse of the infinite, eternal magnitude and omnipotence of All That Is.

Life on earth is not inferior to its non-physical source. We are so pleased to remind you of the divine total being that you are, and of your intention to express that as you eagerly birthed into this joy-filled earth. There is only pain and struggle when you live in fear and resistance and believe you are only physical. Although humans are not as expansive or permanent as their non-physical soul selves, they are nevertheless an extremely valued and important extension of God.

2. Everyone creates his or her reality through the law of attraction and the power of focus and concentration.

You create your reality through thoughts, feelings, emotions, beliefs, and expectations. You are magnets that attract like for like. The people, situations, events, and experiences that are in your life are the reflections of your beliefs and vibrational offerings.

Vibrations are impersonal. You attract what you focus and concentrate on, whether you consider it positive or negative.

3. Life is eternally for you. The universe is safe and abundant.

Life is always for you. It eternally provides you with all the resources you need in order to thrive. Life constantly bends in your direction when you trust and allow the process in joy.

Wellbeing is the rule. Unless you resist the natural flow through fear, doubt, and judgment.

You live in a physical, three-dimensional, polarized, dense reality. You are also a part of an electromagnetic positive and negative reality. This reality consists of contrast such as white and black, dark and light, wellness and illness. Contrast provides the backdrop or options for creation. You may say it contains the building blocks consciousness uses for creation and fulfillment. The natural power of life pulsates through you in a continuous flow unless you restrict it through resistance, fear, and doubt.

All of your individual and societal challenges such as disease, poverty, hatred, war, depression, and lack of joy and fulfillment are the result of powerlessness and ignorance of universal laws. When you do not understand or know this on a mental, spiritual, emotional, and visceral level, you attempt to control, change, or manipulate others through rigid rules, regulations, and laws. You allow external conditions to determine your attitude and your actions.

Real security and safety does not come from the government, military, police or any god outside of you. Freedom, co-operation, and safety are an inherent foundation within all consciousness. Accordingly, your body intrinsically has the capability to function effortlessly. The physical body itself is natural proof of grace. Your entire body is comprised of billions of cellular mini universes that are on some level conscious, all cooperating and communicating with each other. The natural functioning of your body—from your heartbeat to your metabolism— is evidence of how life is for you. You do not have to force or make anything happen. You live in a safe and abundant universe. Since everything is God, there is only well-being, harmony, love, joy, and fulfillment.

Life is supposed to be good. Moreover, you can be, do, or have the essence of anything you desire. However, because freedom is intrinsically the essence of All That Is, each expression of consciousness is free to create, explore, and experience both the positive and negative.

No thing can invade, coerce, interfere, manipulate, or hurt any being without its acquiescence on some level.

Many refer to this as free will. We refer to it as the inherent, protective consciousness of All That Is. We only use the word protective to communicate within your belief system, because the essence of this universal law is that there is absolutely nothing to fear. There are no victims. You are always creating your reality through your thoughts, feelings, and beliefs, whether you are focused in the physical or non-physical.

You live in a thriving, ever-growing, abundant world that is always expanding and resourcing itself. Life in quest of life. Scarcity, suffering, and struggle are a man made and perpetuated phenomenon. We repeat that well-being is the natural state of being and not the exception.

4. The purpose of all consciousness is for the value of fulfillment, exploration, expression, enjoyment, and creation in love and joy.

You are much more than the you that exists in a physical body on a physical planet. You are, at the same time, a non-physical consciousness that desires to express and experience physicality. All beings, as well as other kinds of consciousness, are interconnected and interact with each other in various ways. All beings have an insatiable, natural inclination for creativity, exploration, and self-fulfillment. You have an intrinsic propensity to be true to self, to act on inner preferences and desires that culminate in joy and value fulfillment, not only for you and for your larger soul self, but for the collective All That Is.

Use these Universal Laws. Integrate them into your thinking and feeling patterns. Know your beliefs, and be aware of their relationship with the emotional responses you have from moment to moment to external events and conditions. Since your initial thoughts and habitual emotional responses become your reality, it is imperative that you become more aware of these processes.

Become more conscious of how you think, feel, and respond to concepts and circumstances, and you will soon discover why and how you have created your life up to this point. Be assured that no matter what you have created previously, you have the power, in any given moment, to change and transform your life significantly.

Humans are habitual creatures and have become so outer-directed and dependent on others for approval and validation. We are here to assist you in reclaiming your power, to help you become inner-directed and aligned with your soul self, so you can consciously create all that you desire. No one will ever be led astray by following the natural impulses and inner guidance from the authentic self. By doing this, you will not only empower yourself, but you will benefit and contribute to the greater good of your community, your planet, and All That Is.

CHAPTER 4

God Is All That Is

There is no separation between you and God. When you truly understand this concept, you realize that there is indeed no separation between you and another human being, between you and the beasts, or the flowers, or the earth that you stand upon. Everything you see, feel, and touch is integrated within you. It is all God or All that Is. You may choose to label it whatever you would like, but it is infinite, eternal, and expansiveness. It is unconditional love and acceptance. It is the massive energy generator that is the power source for everything in the universe.

Imagine a universal hose through which an endless source of energy flows. This energy is fueled by unconditional love and pulsates through each inner soul self into the physical self and all of its life's creations. It is the ultimate natural resource necessary to sustain natural well-being in all areas of life. This inexhaustible power is always flowing through every living being. Negative emotion, however, caused by self-doubt, fear, judgment, and feelings of powerlessness creates resistance that can "kink" this universal pipeline inhibiting the free flow of this essential life force.

Consequently, the diminishment of this life energy lowers the person's vibrational frequency. This is what causes disease, despair, unhappiness, disharmony, greed, and a feeling of emptiness. There is not a separate evil or dark force responsible for these things. You determine how this life force flows.

The connection between you and All That Is is the energy essence of creativity. In knowing that there is no separation, you can have everything that you desire. It is all yours when you align with that energy essence. Sometimes, the connection appears to be severed through self-doubt, fear, and uneasiness about ones own self. However, in truth, there is no separation. You are divinely connected to Source Energy, and when you listen to the voice within, that voice that calls you forward, you know this.

You are a loved, cherished, worthy, powerful being that is a valued part of the divine fabric, the All That Is-ness. You, as a microcosm of a dynamic macrocosm, contribute to the overall expansion of All that Is by being your natural self. All That Is grows and expands through the wishes, dreams, ideas, and visions of every human being.

Your personal life emerges out of the greater gestalt of consciousness of your over soul, and your physical desires and materializations add to the exploration and value fulfillment of what you may refer to as God.

Some believe they must be punished now for crimes, sins, or injustices from other lifetimes. On the other hand, that they have to go through several reincarnation cycles in order to "graduate" from the earth plane and go home to the non-physical realms perfect and finished. Some say you were born flawed, sinful, undeserving, or needing to be saved from evil powers or outside forces. The truth is, so-called evil forces are man made, and you are never judged or punished, because ultimately there is no right or wrong, good or bad.

When you truly understand the law of attraction and that you indeed create your reality, you will see that there are no accidents or victims. No one can create in another's consciousness or reality. No person, teacher, or even God, can interfere, coerce, invade, change, or force anyone to do anything without his or her agreement. Free will and freedom are the foundation of all beings.

Everything physical has a larger aspect or non-physical counterpart at its source. However, everything non-physical does not always have a physical counterpart. The non-physical is larger and more permanent, but the physical is not inferior or less important. Earth is an extremely desirable place to be. Earth life is delicious. All physical realities, including earth life, are for the joyful and creative expression of the non-physical being choosing fulfilling experience. It is all a choice. No one is forced into this exciting adventure. All That Is is never finished or complete, because everything is eternally evolving, expanding, and growing. If there were a God that was finished, all universes, physical and non-physical, would cease to be.

To summarize, God or All That Is God is the only power that exists. Within this greater God are trillions of entities or collective consciousnesses composed of many inner selves. These inner selves, or soul selves, have outer physical selves. We are fragmenting these aspects merely for communication purposes. There is no separation between the non-physical and the physical. There are no rules, shoulds, should nots or outside recriminations or punishments, only free choice—awareness or unconsciousness.

QUESTIONS AND ANSWERS

Linda: There are many people I've encountered in my life who feel to me like they are surrendering their power and they just want God to lead them. Can you compare that to us creating our own perceptions of what we want to do as opposed to being led by God? Is there a difference in that?

Orion: It depends on one's idea of what God is. If they are saying that God is something outside of themselves, and they are turning their power over to something they believe to be outside of them, then we would say that is not the perception that we want individuals to have of God. We say that if you are relinquishing your power and turning it over to something outside of yourself, you will have difficulty. When you say you are turning it over to God and you believe that God is something that plays games with your life, or if God is something you feel you need to answer to rather than to be a part of, you are giving your power away. It is when you are in harmony with that God essence—that force, power, being of All That Is, everything that is in existence—it is all connected to you, and there is no separation.

Linda: So if I take that concept one-step further, would it be safe to say that our desires and urges could be the way that the God part of our self communicates to us?

Orion: Yes.

Ken: What would you recommend people do to really comprehend what God is for themselves?

Orion: What we want individuals to do is explore what they perceive their God to be. We hope that they will understand that the God they listen to is within them rather than outside of themselves. The perception or connection individuals have to the God/Goddess essence energy will effect how they see themselves, the world, and everything in existence. They may call it God or Goddess, All That Is, Buddha, Jesus, or Mohammed. It really matters not from our perspective. We only want each individual to find that connection to the Source that lies within. Therefore, whatever they deem it to be really matters not, only that they discover it for themselves.

If they have a perception of God in which they are not a participant, they will see God as something separate or outside of themselves, something to worship or pray to. We want them to reflect that back to themselves as a mirror image. If you are worshiping or praying to a God that lies somewhere other than within, you should put the mirror of life to your face. What do you see? It is the reflection of what God is. That reflection of God is you and your participation with life.

Ken: How does our divine connection apply in everyday activities?

Orion: When you are truly connected, truly feeling that divine energy resonating from the bottom of your toes to the top of your head, you feel exhilaration. You feel excitement. You feel joyful. You feel that orgasmic feeling of life. Just as babies express their joy with each new pleasure that comes to them—the touch of their own foot, flickering lights—they become excited by the life force around them. The universal energy of All That Is is expressed through you, as you, in you. Be at peace and enjoy that expression of you, and your participation with life. That is the God connection.

Linda: The concept that there is no place that God is not and that we are an expression or reflection of God is hard for many to grasp. That is a profound concept or image.

Orion: There is so much emphasis on the word God, and because religions have placed a lot of importance on the word God, it often gets misconstrued. God is Universal Intelligence, and you are all connected to it. You come into this physical reality as a thread, an extension of that Universal Intelligence. Everything you see, touch, smell, and discover is Universal Intelligence. It is everything and nothing. Everything is an expression of that which people have deemed to be God. We would prefer to erase the word God and merely say that everything—every plant, pebble, speck of sunlight, rainbow, flower, tree, human, etc.—is an expression of that Universal Intelligence.

Experience life from the perspective of being connected to everything. Observe and experience life from your sensory perceptions. Feel, touch and smell everything—the creatures, storms, sunrises, sunsets, the earth as you walk. As you drive in your automobiles, look around and observe life expressing itself. You are connected to all of it.

It is indeed a difficult concept for people to understand they are God. If you can get past the label of what God has come to mean, we believe you would once again feel and sense everything in existence, bring it into your bodies, and feel the connection. When you have a tear in your eye, when you feel goose bumps, when you feel a smile or sadness coming on, or when you look at nature and see the beautiful birds and butterflies flying about enjoying themselves, that is each of you being in the flow of life. No matter what you are expressing at any given moment, you are Life, God, Universal Intelligence expressing through your senses.

Ken: Is that what Jesus was saying when he said, "Be still and know that I am God?" That there is no separation? He was not just talking about himself personally, was he?

Orion: Precisely. He was speaking to the masses saying be still and know you are God. You are all expressions as we just rambled on about, expressions of life, expressions of what is in existence, expressions of Universal Intelligence. Be still and know you are all Gods and Goddesses.

Linda: And plants and animals are God. Some expressions are more expanded or evolved than others, but everything is God. Right?

Orion: Yes. Everything is God.

Linda: So it is not sacrilegious to say that a dog is also God.

Orion: And when you spell God backwards, what do you have?

Ken: Just like evil. When you spell evil backwards, you have "live." So essentially evil is, in essence, exactly that—when you are not living and affirming life, correct?

Orion: If you must think that there is evil at all. Of course, we do not think that there is evil.

Ken: Would you say that most of the guilt, judgment, shame, and blame came from our religions?

Orion: Indeed. Religion was brought about through man's perception. Through religion, individuals could be controlled by fear and guilt. If you did not do certain things, it was a sin. Consequently, if you were a sinner, you must go to church and give your money so your feelings of guilt and shame and fear and doubt could be taken away.

However, you are all connected to Universal Intelligence and Universal Intelligence knows no "no," it knows no wrong, it knows no evil, it knows no bad or sin

When religions began telling children to believe in the dogma they wanted them to believe in, without thinking, without questioning, that is where the problems started. Individuals laid down their lives for these churches and religions that were created by man's perception of what they deemed were God's word. Individuals followed what they were told and did not question. Without questioning, they were led down the road to whatever religion seemed to fit at a given moment in time.

However, we want you to discover for yourselves what it was within you that drew you into that perception of what those individuals led you to believe was God. Question and discover for yourself. Look inside and peel the layers. Find what lies within. What you will discover is that there is nothing but good, nothing but well-being. That is the source of God/Universal Intelligence/All That Is.

Linda: It is so hard for many people, especially older people, to not believe in evil.

Orion: Yes, they have been so inundated with these concepts repeatedly for years that they cannot break this habit of thinking. Moreover, it is just that—a habit of thinking, a habit of belief—that they have given themselves over to without questioning that belief. They believe that what is being told to them is something they are not supposed to question. They believe this is the gospel according to God, and they cannot look within. They are so frightened to look at themselves and discover who they are and actually free themselves from that burden of fear and doubt and sin. It is senseless for an individual to believe that there would be such a God who would give them this burden of sin and guilt and fear. There is only well-being. When an individual learns that, they will feel light.

There are individuals who will never want to peel away those layers, and that is perfectly fine. They are happy with being led and being told how to live their lives. There are different perceptions, different ways of living, and different ways of looking at life. We place no judgment on how anyone wants to live. We are merely here to show you that there is only well-being. When you feel that lightness within, where there is no guilt or doubt or fear or sin, you can breathe easy. You shoulders will lift, and you will feel light and free.

Linda: I think because of the Bible or what is written in the Bible, many people do not question. They believe that what was written in the Bible is the word of God, the absolute truth. Can you speak to that?

Orion: If we told you it was channeled material, most of you would find that amazing. However, in essence, that is what it is. Individuals will discover for themselves that the Bible has had many translations and many perceptions of what the words mean to them. You could have twenty-five people reading that book and you would have twenty-five different perceptions of each sentence. What we want to convey is it matters not what your perception of those words are. If you believe it to be the word of God, so be it. You will see that there are even different ministers who will have their own take on those words. They can play them out however they choose for their congregation. Therefore, it is even better if an individual has no perception of what God is.

If an individual has a deep-seated perception of God and religion, we say believe what you want to believe, it makes no difference to us. Nevertheless, what we want to convey to you is that if you read those words from the concept that there is only good, only well-being, then you will see that there is only well-being being written. It is your perception of the words, your perception coming from your belief system. If you have a belief system that there is evil, that there is sin, or that God should be feared, then that is what you will see being written. We really have no easy answers for everyone, except for them to discover for themselves what feels best to them.

Ken: So many religious and spiritual teachings are about forgiveness.

Orion: Yes, oftentimes, individuals do not forgive themselves for past things, and it does no good to harbor hard feelings or to continually beat up on yourself over something that has happened in the past. It is just that. It is in your past, and the point of power is *now*. Ultimately, there is nothing to forgive, since there are no absolute good, bad, right, wrong or victims. However, if you believe in good and evil and victimhood, then forgiveness is beneficial, especially forgiving of self.

Ken: When we really begin to understand that we create our reality, that there are no victims, and realize that no one can do anything to us, the only person to forgive is ourselves.

Orion: Indeed. Love yourself always. It is so important to understand that you create your reality, because guilt is a habitual emotional response. You created a learned response because of what you were taught by all the well-intentioned authority figures in your lives. It takes time to unlearn that and become more inner directed. When you intellectually understand this and the natural laws, you still have to re-train your whole nervous system and your habitual emotional responses.

Not only do you have to intellectually grasp the natural laws and understand that there aren't conditions or things that you have to do to correct or change your outer circumstances, but you have to, in tandem, viscerally feel that everything is within your consciousness to change and create.

Ken: So no matter what turmoil or strife we may face— whether it has to do with money or relationships, whether it is strangers, relatives, or friends—no one can fix or solve our challenges for us. Everything is a do-it-yourself process, correct?

Orion: It is an inside job, indeed. When you change the way you look at things and how you have looked at things through your eyes, through your beliefs, everything in your reality changes. When you realize that through your belief system you have created everything in your life, you begin to become conscious or deliberate with your thoughts. Learn to believe in yourself and trust your inner guidance, your inner knowing. Trust yourself and know that what you choose for yourself is of the most benefit to you at any particular time.

Linda: And wherever you are in your evolution of beliefs, you can trust and allow that place on your path. Even if your beliefs are limiting and not highly evolved, you can still trust in your own unique way. Do you know what I am trying to say?

Orion: Yes we do. So no matter where you are in your evolution of your beliefs—perhaps you are still examining your beliefs, or perhaps you are still exchanging beliefs because you are still learning about self—you are always learning, expanding, growing, experimenting, and having fun in life. No matter what part of your evolution you are in, you can indeed see and believe in yourself and your intuition, and know that life is unfolding naturally effortlessly, endlessly.

CHAPTER 5

Life is for You

Imagine a bird sitting peacefully soaking up the energy of what is and then suddenly taking flight. He looks around at nothing in particular, and merely takes off and enjoys the flight. The bird enjoys what is. The bird feels the wind and co-operates with it. It flies with the wind current and allows the wind to carry it. As he soars about the sky, he encompasses the feeling of freedom. The flight is a symbol of nothing and yet everything.

Human beings should see themselves as birds in flight allowing the wind and the air currents to carry them along. Look up in the sky and admire the wingspan of a glorious bird. See it soaring effortlessly, enjoying itself and its flight for what it is as it is carried from place to place. As it soars, it allows the wind to carry it along its path, just as you all do when you trust and allow life to support you and life's creative and powerful flow of energy to flow through you as you.

You are it. You are the ones allowing, being, doing, thinking, and feeling. Allow yourselves the freedom to be, do, and have. Imagine life, as you desire it to be, and allow life to carry you along a beautiful journey. Often in the great adventure, you will find yourselves changing paths, changing directions, changing the way you look at things, and changing your visions.

Changing as you go allows life to carry you along with it. When you relax and enjoy this stream of energy, which is you, and enjoy who you are without the expectations of others, you allow yourself the freedom to think and to experience life the way you choose to. You are always growing and always looking forward with much eagerness. This great adventure gets even more exciting and fulfilling when you trust and allow the process of life in joy and when you are true to yourself. Allow the spirit within to take flight, to experience the effortless journey of joy, happiness, and fulfillment as you allow yourself the freedom to be who you are.

You will continue to gain power and strength within as you become more aware of that spirit of self, that spirit that you came forth from. Continue to enjoy the merging of the creative life force that is your physical self with the powerful, inexhaustible, loving, larger non-physical part of you. Be aware of your built-in freedom to either allow or pinch off the well-being that always flows. Understand that because freedom is the basis of the universe, limiting beliefs of fear and unworthiness may prevent you from the rightful inheritance All That Is is eternally showering upon you—that of joy, abundance, health, and fulfillment.

When you trust and allow the process of life, when you find your wings once again and see yourself soaring and believing in self, and when you make peace with what is and enjoy the journey wherever if finds you, you will see the beauty and glory in life. Even when things seem to be difficult or appear to be challenging, do not give up on your dreams, wishes, and desires. Challenge is a part of the journey. However, we remind you that the journey of life is beautiful and fulfilling when you trust and allow the process in joy.

Allow nature to be your teacher. Observe how every life form, by being its unique self, contributes to the co-creation of everything else, which culminates in natural abundance, beauty, and well-being forever expanding All That Is.

Enjoy the spontaneity and the synchronicities that deliciously present themselves. Enjoy each and every being and all of the beasts. Enjoy what is, for it is indeed a part of you. Feel the energies of life in you. Feel yourself soaring and envisioning all the wonderful things you desire. Feel the wind caressing you beneath your wings. Soar once again with ease and delight and know that life is for you!

QUESTIONS AND ANSWERS

Ken: If we really believed and lived life knowing that life is for us, would we totally trust and allow? Would we have an abundant and joy-filled life?

Orion: We assure you that life is for you. We assure you that abundance; well-being, joy, contentment, and fulfillment are all yours. If you believed that there was only well-being, and if you could walk through life knowing, believing, and trusting this with every fiber of your being, that would be your experience.

Ken: So whenever conditions in our life are less than desirable, like sickness, relationship problems, financial problems, or feelings of any kind of pain, depression, or lack of fulfillment, is it because there is at least one universal law that we do not viscerally believe? We might intellectually believe it, but not viscerally?

Orion: Yes. That or you have completely kinked off your connection to your larger soul self. You have put a crimp in that hose of well-being. Therefore, if you have put a crimp in that hose of well-being, of course you are going to come up against this friction, against this not believing in self, not trusting in life, not knowing that all is well. When you have kinked that off, you will indeed draw into your life those things that are not desirable.

Linda: I would also like to add that not only is life always for us, but it is always calling us forward. Moreover, if we listen, we can follow the calling. Could you explain how we can better listen?

Orion: Yes. Everyone gets so wrapped up in day-to-day activities. They have so much going on in their lives that they have forgotten to take a moment as you all did earlier. You were all standing on the balcony and breathing in the beautiful air and feeling the energy of the storm and feeling the freshness of the breeze and of the raindrops. You stood there and took in all of life. You were taking the time to do nothing and everything by enjoying the moment.

Each individual could take five minutes to stop and do nothing. Take a deep breath, observe your surroundings, close your eyes if only for a moment and realize that life is indeed calling you forward, there is no turning back, there is only movement forward. Take a brief five minutes out of your busy schedule to take that deep breath, to open your eyes, feel, breathe, and smell the earth. Enjoy those moments expressing yourself as you. Express yourself as the beautiful being that you are, and again feel the aliveness of that.

Linda: We are really our own worst enemy—whatever division or separation we feel, or whatever suffering we feel.

Orion: It is all done by self. Get out of your own way and enjoy life. Observe yourself and your reactions. Learn from what you speak, how you react, and how you interact with others. As you observe yourself, through all of life's wonderful gifts that it gives you, you become more consciously aware of your habitual thought patterns. As you become more aware of your thought patterns, you then can change them. As you become more aware of your thought patterns and your responses and reactions to what life gives you, you can put the pieces of the puzzle together and say, "Yes, I have created that. Yes, I am creating as I go. I am changing my life as I go, as I learn, as I observe, as I feel."

Ken: What is the practical value of knowing that life is always for you?

Orion: When you absolutely know that life is for you and have integrated it into your conscious awareness, then your life can be safe, healthy and joyful. Life always responds to your thoughts, words, deeds, and feelings. When you honestly evaluate your habitual, emotional response patterns, you will discover that much of what is undesirable in your life is the result of your habitual ingrained beliefs that life is not always for you, but is a struggle or hard. Therefore, once you understand how your daily life is the mirror of your attitudinal vibration, you will want to focus more on all the evidence that life is always supporting and prospering those who think, feel, respond, and act from their natural selves.

Ken: So essentially you are saying that we do live in a safe and abundant universe and that since we are physicalized aspects of God, then it is only natural that life is eternally for us.

Orion: Although your world may reflect unsafe, unhealthy, or impoverished attitudinal vibrations, if you could change your thinking and feeling patterns in yourself, you would see that life is and has been trying to support you. However, because of your fear and doubt you do not see or attract the opportunities that support that. For every obstacle that your sabotaging fear beliefs may attract, the universe is always trying to provide you with another more positive solution.

Linda: In our society, it often looks like bad things just happen to people.

Orion: Everything is lining up for you. All possibilities positive and negative are dangling out there in response to you. It's the one that is living the life that is either letting their desires in or not. Your habitual response patterns will usual bring you more of the same. Because most are focused on external circumstances, they don't realize or they forget that they create the experience, not that others or outside events create them. So from within to the outer you create, not the other way around. If your life has many challenges, you probably have allowed outside forces to control you. You are the control tower beaming out signals, which are your feelings and beliefs.

CHAPTER 6

Cosmic Vibrators and Human Magnets

Before this session began, Leslie noticed the hummingbirds finding their way to the feeder on the porch. The hummingbirds were flapping their wings, but you could not see them do this, because they were moving at such a high rate of speed. You all are cosmic vibrators, in a sense, flapping your wings at a high rate of speed. You and everything in your world is pulsating in and out of your reality so fast that it all appears to be solid and constant. Every person, place, or thing, including all particles, has their own rate and degree of vibration.

Everything in the cosmos, from the infinitesimal microscopic organisms in a pond, through the rocks, trees, humans, and animals on earth, to the furthest galaxies has consciousness that consists of electromagnetic vibrational energy. All consciousness—physical and non-physical—has various levels and ranges of vibrational frequency. All thoughts emit a vibrational signal that attracts other vibrational frequencies that match them.

We have told you before that you are more than the physical flesh, blood, and body. Your earth self is only one aspect of you. Again, we tell you that you are both physical and non-physical at the same time. You are made up of inaudible sound and invisible light and vibrational frequencies that are pulsating at tremendous speed. Much like your planet, which from your perspective appears to be stationary, you are spinning in your orbit.

Your entire world, the entire universe is vibrational in nature. Being that vibrational energy, the law of attraction naturally governs everything in your world. The law of attraction is an equal opportunity manager. In other words, the law of attraction is impersonal. It works the same for everyone no matter how rich or poor, what nationality, religion, or gender they are. Because of this law of attraction, your thoughts and feelings attract those people, experiences, and events that correspond with those vibrations.

Your day-to-day reality, including your health, finances, relationships, and circumstances, are the reflections of your thoughts, feelings, intents, expectations, desires, and your emotional reactions and responses. They determine vibrational frequencies. Your life is like a movie or a play in which you are the playwright, actor, and director. Behind the scenes is an invisible universal casting studio casting all the parts. This casting studio can be thought of as the law of attraction headquarters. It manages and facilitates all the vibrational enactments from every one and everything in order that all vibrational offerings match.

Therefore, your thoughts, desires, dreams, and fears have vibrations that are electromagnetically broadcasted out via this casting studio where the casting call goes out for all the characters, events, and circumstances that manifest in your daily life. Those manifestations are always a vibrational equivalent to your thoughts and feelings.

You are a transmitter and receiver broadcasting your attitudinal vibrational signals every moment of your life. Your thoughts and feelings are magnets of energy in motion that attract like for like. Positive thoughts and emotions attract positive outcomes. Negative thoughts and feelings draw to you negative outcomes. Every creation has its vibrational root. Be aware of how your feelings reflect your energy and broadcast it outward.

Even when things do not appear to be going as hoped, you are creating the life of your choosing. It may not be a conscious choice, but events are indeed being drawn to you through the thoughts and vibrational feeling tones you have sent out to the universe. When life appears to be a tangled mess, and you wonder where it's coming from, we assure you that it is coming from you. You may be putting up resistance that you're not even aware of. When you relax and allow life to flow through you effortlessly and joyously, things becomes much easier. Life is always conspiring to shower each of you with all the necessary resources for prosperity, health, and joy-filled experiences.

You attract what you concentrate on. Learn to relax and use your imagination to focus on your intentions and desires. Then allow your emotions to intensify those intentions, and the law of attraction will propel them from your inner world to your outer world. When you concentrate on what you do not want, or what you fear, that is what will manifest in your reality. Nevertheless, do not condemn yourself for negative thoughts and emotions and the circumstances that they create, but realize that they are barometers and can be changed.

Listen to the conversations you have with others and with yourself, and guide your negative thoughts and emotions into positive thoughts and emotions. Your emotions will follow your thoughts and beliefs. Simultaneously, observe your habitual emotional responses to other people and outer circumstances in your life.

If you want to change your life, change your beliefs. Do a review of your past and you will most likely see many repeated patterns of life experiences. Think of friends, relatives, and the various patterns that you have seen repeated in their lives. Observe your life now—the work place, the news, your relatives, and social life—and once again you will see patterns of repeated behavior and results. How many end a relationship with a person acting out a particular tendency that creates conflict only to eventually end up in the subsequent relationship with a different person that has the same trait. Notice that people who call themselves "accident prone," have accidents. Or how those whose conversations are mostly about illness are usually sickly.

Your beliefs, feelings, and expectations create your day-to-day experience. The law of attraction responds to the vibrational attitudinal equivalent of each person's habitual, emotional responses to life. This is evident to a large extent in the area of money and career. The rich get richer and the poor get poorer. Those with perpetual financial challenges often have the belief that life is a struggle. Those who are seriously overweight cannot see or think of themselves any other way. You get what your focus upon.

How does a belief start? How can you change one belief into another? What is the inside work that needs to be done? How can you learn to look at things differently, to feel things differently?

First, you must clearly understand that your outer life is a reflection of your beliefs. When you see that you are receiving a result that you no longer want, something in what you are focusing upon must change so that your situation will have a different outcome. Become aware of your habitual emotional responses. Change your perceptions of situations you do not want by looking for the underlying belief. Change that belief and you will change your vibrational frequency and start to see a different result. Then you can determine if this new result is something you want. If you are in harmony with this new manifestation or circumstance, then continue to hold your new perceptions, feelings, and responses.

This is a process, and by taking small incremental steps towards changing your beliefs, gradually your responses, both in emotion and in action, will correspond with your new perspective. You have the power, as human magnets, to intentionally attract the life of your choice.

QUESTIONS AND ANSWERS

Ken: Can you talk a little more about the universal casting studio?

Orion: The casting studio is a metaphor for the non-physical vibrational energy that manages everyone's desires, and dreams. An invisible studio, if you will, that will match, coordinate, and manage the alignment and synchronization of those events and experiences that will manifest on life's physical stage. Remember, everything physical has a non-physical counterpart. Therefore, you may say that your casting studio arranges everything. Therefore, all you have to do is give a clear intent and the casting studio will work out the details.

Linda: So what happens when the person changes his or her mind?

Orion: The inexhaustible vibrational realms of the casting studio will shift, always reflecting the current desires and expectations.

Linda: Can you further explain the law of attraction.

Orion: It's like a magnetic pull. If you have a negative and a positive like the poles of a magnet, and if you place the magnets in certain positions they will either attract or repel. It is that way with the law of attraction. Your thoughts and feelings emit electromagnetic energy and as you send out particular thoughts, you either attract or repel conditions and experiences that match your thoughts. Those thought, intents, desires, fears, expectations become your emotions, your energies in motion. You attract what you want and viscerally believe you can have, and repel what you feel you cannot attract for many reasons according to your beliefs and expectations. You will attract whatever you concentrate on and believe. For instance, Linda, when you kept saying that one day you would meet President Obama and shake his hand, how did the universe respond? Yes, you aligned with just the right connections to enable you to greet and meet the president and shake his hand. Think of all the many synchronicities, such as working with a person who knew one of the secret service personnel who would be on duty the day the President would be visiting Dayton, Ohio and your workmate would ask you if you would like to meet the President! Doesn't that sound astonishing? In reality though, you knew that one day somehow, you would meet the President!

Ken: So you can also attract the opposite of what you want if you are focused on something but don't think you can have it. Maybe you don't feel deserving.

Orion: Yes. Also, if you are thinking a lot about making money, but you are focusing on poverty or a recession, in other words lack, you will attract shortage.

Linda: Did you say earlier that everything in the cosmos is vibrating, even non-humans?

Orion: Yes, this is a vibrational universe. All animals, insects, plants, trees, rocks, soil, and stars are vibrational in nature.

Linda: Do animals create their reality?

Orion: Yes, although beasts don't reflect or have the same intellectual capabilities. They are more instinctual. They follow inner guidance. The beasts are definitely less resistant than humans are. However, the same natural universal laws also apply to them. On certain levels, they choose their conditions and birth and will exit this reality when they are ready. All of these decisions are made in harmonious cooperation with every other living and non-living thing.

Ken: How do beliefs enter in this law of attraction process?

Orion: You create your reality based on your beliefs, feelings, and expectations. Beliefs are strong ideas, you may say convictions, that create various emotions and produce an electromagnetic reality. The law of attraction works by charging these ideas and emotions with energy that will be emitted and received like for like. Therefore, you may say that a part of the function of the law of attraction serves as a control tower that acts as a sender and receiver of electromagnetically charged conscious and telepathic data.

It is like the remote control that operates the television set. To tune into a particular channel, you set the device and the set signal goes out searching for that particular station. The garage door opener is another example of sending out the message from your remote to the garage that has a receiving mechanism to open the door.

CHAPTER 7

Safe and Abundant Universe

As you look out your window on a snowy evening, you see an abundance of white, fluffy flakes. As you look at the natural world, it is abundant with trees, flowers, and creatures. The abundance of this reality is everywhere. Be grateful for the abundance in life, in *your* life. Be grateful for being alive, for being as you are. Abundance is not only about wealth. It is everything that exists in the universe.

Become aware of how you keep your personal prosperity from yourself. Listen to your words, expressions, and responses. Listen to others in day-to-day conversations. Be aware of the flow of currency in exchange for goods and services. Listening to others can sometimes make the connection between what one believes and speaks and what one receives clearer to you. As you listen and observe, you will begin to see how some individuals create more prosperity than others do.

Look at your own beliefs. What are your thoughts, words, and fears about prosperity and abundance? We merely want you to be aware. Be aware of how you speak your words. Observe how you converse in a store, how you speak with your loved ones, or with co-workers. It will become quite clear to you what your own prosperity and abundance consciousness is.

Be aware of so-called obsessive-compulsive behavior. This is a mindset of fear or lack. When you are overly obsessive about something, you are in the mindset of constantly thinking *Am I doing it enough? Am I doing it correctly? Am I in the sequence? Am I in the flow? Do I trust my inner guidance and myself?* When you trust, allow, know, and believe in your self, you are indeed in the flow of everything. You know that all is well, that all is in divine order.

You are responsible for your experience of life to the fullest extent. You are responsible for your life in everything that it encompasses. Your placement in the universe or your state of being is up to you. What is it that you want to experience? How do you want to see yourself? It is how you feel about yourself, whether or not you feel worthy, and how aligned you are with what you want that determines your state of being and your experiences. Do you see yourself in a world of abundance or in a world of lack? Do you find yourself in a world of happiness and joy, or in a world of sadness and sorrow? Do you see yourself with love and self-acceptance, or do you focus on all of the negative aspects of self? This is all a part of feeling safe and abundant.

You all want to be expressive and empowered individual beings that know no boundaries. And we want to say to you that you are all living this now. You are all expressing yourselves as individuals, free to think the thoughts you think and question those ideas that do not make sense to you. Some of you may ask, "How do I express myself without all of the baggage I carry with me?" We say to you— put down those bags, for they no longer need to be with you.

It is time now to be the fullest expression of your soul self and to live the life you choose to live. You are free. You can be free of all the hurt, the anger, the disappointments, and the disparaging words. You are free from those individuals who said that you will never amount to anything or those who asked, "Who do you think you are?" Today is your day. You are here. You are full of questions. You are full of interest. You are excited to be creating the life of choice and you are looking forward to so much more.

Live your lives by expressing yourselves from the inside out. Express yourselves fully and completely and let down your armor. Let others see you as you are—a creative, beautiful expression of life here in this time-space reality for a reason. You are here to fully express yourselves and to feel the power within, the power that has always been there.

Your connection does indeed often times become disconnected when you listen to those who like to pick at you and try to take pieces of you. After a while, you feel like there is nothing left of the you that you came here to be. Come back to yourself. Come back to that energy within, that connection to All That Is.

By being here and by being a part of this leading edge and by being a part of All That Is, you can feel yourselves becoming more powerful from the inside out, through the connection you all have to the energy that exists throughout the universe. Plug in. Trust that life is for you and allow yourselves that freedom and knowing of who you are, what you are, and what you want to express yourself as. Express yourselves and fear not what anyone else thinks. Be who you want to be and love yourselves.

As you go through your everyday life, you may find yourself in a conversation with someone where a hot topic may come up about politics or religion, and you want to convince the other person that your point of view is better. We will say to you, don't get caught up in who is right and who is wrong. That just feeds into more of what you don't want. Believe that your world is full of love and peace and harmony and that all is well. For really, all is well, whether it be perceived from the eyes of someone that sees war as being necessary, or from the eyes of someone that sees war as against everything they believe in. It is in those moments that you need to remind yourself that you indeed have the power to choose to be happy with your perspective. If you do this and allow others to believe as they choose, then all is well.

When individuals push your buttons and irritate you, if is because you have allowed them to. You must remind yourself that you are a powerful, loving, self-directed, self-knowing individual who sees a world where there is love, peace, harmony, and beauty regardless of any outer circumstance. Be happy in your life and allow others to be happy in theirs. You have the freedom to be who you are and the freedom to choose to remain silent or unaffected by outer circumstances. When you are truly connected, all is perfect, whole, and complete.

We would like to say something about faith and trust. These words are interchangeable. Faith is when you have the inner knowing that you indeed can trust what you believe. Let us say, for example, that you believe that all is well and connected in the sense that you are part of Source Energy or All That Is, that that divine connection is never broken, that all is well. It would follow that if you believed this, then you believe in a universe that is safe. Therefore, if someone knocked at your door, you would approach the door knowing there is nothing there that will harm you.

If, however, you believed that the universe was *not* safe and there were harmful beings roaming the streets, and someone approached your door, you could be harmed. Because of the vibration you are putting out, among the thousands of doors in the city, the harm-doer would find yours. Like attracts like. The fear of harm and the intention to harm someone have the same vibrational attraction. If you truly believe that this is a safe universe, then it is indeed a safe universe, and nothing will harm you.

QUESTIONS AND ANSWERS

Linda: You have said that there are no accidents or victims, and that so-called victims attract disasters because of beliefs. Many people may misunderstand and think you are saying they wanted to be sick or robbed.

Orion: No, that is rarely the case. Most people are not aware of their belief systems or their constant fearful self-talk. The law of attraction ensures that thoughts, feelings, and beliefs of positive expectation will draw positive people and experiences, and negative or fearful beliefs and expectations will attract negative or fearful people and circumstances. Very few people want to be sick, poor, assaulted, abused, or unhappy. Most, however, live their lives unconscious of their beliefs. Yet, more and more are learning about the natural universal laws.

Ken: Many people today are fearful of things like natural disasters and limited resources.

Orion: If an individual is drawn to a particular limiting belief, that limiting belief is a part they have not yet discovered about themselves. As you all continue on your quest, there will always be individuals who have fears of things like germs, demons, devils, and such. So be it. You all have to discover for yourself that these are your beliefs. It is as you say a do-it-yourself project. There is nothing that anyone can say to an individual or do for an individual who is not ready to move forward.

In this self-discovery journey, for some people there will be challenges along the way. In your physical reality, there will always be a variety of spiritual, religious, or societal beliefs for you to ponder and that you will be drawn to. This is all part of your self-discovery journey, and we are hopeful that individuals will eventually discover that life is for them, that there is only well-being, and that life is grand and glorious. When you tap into that energy that is always a part of you and never separate from you, you will reunite with your larger whole self and the well-being.

Linda: I have some questions about the whole abundance and prosperity issue. I get confused sometimes when I see people who have money, but who don't think they're rich, and others who don't have money, but appear to feel wealthy and happy.

I know that everything is relative, but I'm curious to know how someone who doesn't have a prosperity consciousness attracts money to begin with. Could it be that in financially wealthy families, the children naturally expect or pick up this prosperity consciousness because that's what they see? Whereas children from lower socio-economic families who don't see financial abundance or have this model don't learn it or visualize prosperity in that respect. It just seems like there are a lot of different ways to pick up a prosperity consciousness.

Orion: It is all of that. When you observe someone who has financial wealth that you believe does not have a prosperity consciousness, we assure you that they do, or they would not have what they have. When they appear to be clutching on to what they have or hoarding or hanging on to what they have for fear that there will not be enough, we assure you that their desires preceded what they have. Their desires had already gone out to the universe, and they have aligned with them, often even unbeknownst to themselves. It is in those desires that it first began.

When you observe individuals that have money or prosperity—whatever you deem that to be—and you wonder how it happened, often it happened as a wee one when they first arrived here on earth. They came from that consciousness when they arrived, so those desires were set forth from the beginning. But if life shows them that money is not good, they may either lose what they have, or never acquire what they had sent out to the universe, or other circumstances may take place.

Ken: And the fulfillment derived from those manifestations is relative to an individual's prosperity consciousness.

Orion: Yes.

Ken: Because someone who society might say is living an impoverished life may be flourishing from a feeling of fulfillment, while someone who has millions may not be enjoying it for fear of losing it.

Linda: It's difficult for me to understand how some people can attract lots of money if they are fearful of losing it or obsessed about having enough.

Ken: You just answered your own question. You didn't have that desire initially.

Orion: It does not mean that you cannot change your belief system about it.

Linda: I just think it is a little confusing sometimes when you say to look at other people to see who has a prosperity consciousness. Because there are people who are tight with their money, or not consciously easy going or free flowing about it yet they have lots of money.

Ken: My definition of someone with a prosperity consciousness though is not necessarily someone with a lot of money. It is someone who spends whatever they need and they do not worry about it and they have whatever they need.

Orion: Prosperity consciousness can be health. It can be happiness, or walking gaily down the street, skipping lightly, or enjoying life, smelling the flowers and smiling. It is all a part of it. It does not necessarily mean how much is in your bank account.

Some individuals love to give back to society. To them that is prosperity—being able to give back because of what they have been given. It is important that individuals give back to the universe in a way that is uniquely fulfilling to them. Some may find fulfillment in cooking bread and cookies and giving them to a neighbor. Some may find that being a volunteer or working with the homeless is gratifying and fulfilling, and that may be their prosperity consciousness. Whatever makes you feel fulfilled and joyful and happy, that is prosperity consciousness. Feeling secure with oneself. Knowing, trusting and being pleased with oneself.

It matters not that someone has $50 in their bank account, or $500,000, or $5 million. It matters only that you are fulfilled.

Linda: Many people fear not having enough money. Security is important, and that's what having money in the bank provides. Security or your bank account in a way can be an obsessive-compulsive issue. It's an artificial sense of security from the fear of not having enough.

Orion: If you trust and believe and know your own power and your own capabilities, you are a prosperous being. Know that all is available to you by tapping in and connecting, as we said earlier, to your whole self. There is no scarcity in the universe. This knowing comes from within. Those thoughts that you cannot make enough money, that you cannot make it on your own are all limiting beliefs in your mind. Once you become self-knowing, self-assured, self- directed, self-reliant, and self-empowered there is no lack. Prosperity comes from within.

Let's say, for example, that you have decided to walk away from everything that you have at this point. You have decided that you are going to start over from scratch. If you have fears and doubts behind that decision, we assure you there will be challenges. If you are fully engaged in the belief that you can indeed make it on your own, you can. If you believe totally in yourself and in your self-reliance, and that you can indeed prosper and be who you want to be and do what you want to do without boundaries, we assure you that it can be.

Ken: Charles Filmore, who founded the Unity Church, said that we increase whatever we praise. Whatever is praised and blessed multiplies. That's why it is so important to count your blessings. Additionally, it is important to make peace with what is. When we are grateful, is it our focus or concentration that is beneficial, or is there something in the art of appreciation itself that is beneficial?

Orion: It is a balance of both. When you focus on what you are grateful for, no matter what it is, you feel at one with those things that you most appreciate. When you are focused and are in that mode of appreciation, you are not thinking of lack. You are not thinking of anything that you do not have, but you are only thinking and appreciating everything that you do have. So it is the focusing that indeed helps to increase your own capability of seeing all of the beautiful things in your lives.

Ken: Would you say that the belief in scarcity is probably one of the largest vibrational causes of many of humanity's problems?

Orion: It is indeed one of the largest causes, as well as not accepting self, not loving self, not being at one with who you are and accepting who you are regardless of what anyone else has fed you about yourself. It is your impression of yourself, of who you are and what you deserve.

See yourself in a deserving mode. You are the one that sees everything in your universe. You see everything that is in your existence. Align yourself with your larger self and the knowledge that you are a divine, creative being. Accept that divine love that is you. Love and accept who you are and that you have the ability to do anything that you desire. Anything that you desire is within arms reach.

It is all a part of it. If you believe that there is lack, that there is something to worry about, that there is not enough of something regardless of what it is—health, money, the air you breathe, food on your table, whatever it is—then you have aligned yourself with a belief in scarcity. When you begin to love and accept yourself and know that you are a divine being that has the energy essence of All That Is, you will find yourself more in control of who you are. When you feel that connection, that connection to everything that exists, you are at one with All That Is. And how wonderful is that?

CHAPTER 8

The Turn-Around Solution

If you have found your way to this information, it is no accident. You are most likely here because you have a quest—a quest for understanding the soul self, the authentic self, that beautiful self. You are all a part of the energy essence of All That Is. You may call it God or Source Energy. You may call it whatever you choose. What matters is that you realize there is no separation between you and that energy. When you do, you will know how powerful and creative you are. You can create the existence that you choose by tapping into that powerful beingness of you that is always there.

If something comes up in your life that feels unbalanced or off kilter and you are not sure why or how it happened, what do you do? Do you keep harboring those same feelings? Do you keep running it through your mind? Do you keep telling everyone the same story? Do you go to a therapist to find out what happened? Do you gather your friends and say, "You know this awful thing happened, and I want you to join me in my misery and sorrow and in this deep hole that I'm digging myself into."

You can stand there and wallow in all of that muck and mire, or you can turn it around. You can accept responsibility for creating the situation. You can begin to look at it differently and start thinking different thoughts. You can begin from right where you are.

Ask yourself where it is you want to go, what it is you want to create in your life. Is it more of what you have right now or is it something different? You get to choose in each moment of each day. You will become more at ease with life when you realize you are the creator. As you create, you expand your conscious awareness of yourself.

All of you have your own stories. All of you have your own dreams, wishes, and desires. All of you perhaps have been in some of those holes that you have dug for yourselves. Now you can see life differently. You can change your thoughts, and as you change your thoughts, you change what is. Your thoughts do the creating. As you think, so shall it be. As you learn more about yourself, your true self, you come to see what a powerful creator you are.

.As you go through life, indeed sometimes you are tripped up. Sometimes you do have a little stumble here and there, but that is fine. Pick yourself up, look around, and find something in front of you to enjoy. Enjoy the connection to Mother Earth. Enjoy the connection with your friends and family and loved ones. Enjoy being here now, on this planet, at this time, experiencing life as you choose to experience it, right here, right now. See yourself growing, expanding, and viewing things differently.

Experience life for the pure joy of it. Experience life in whatever manner you choose. If you want to embark on a different path, to change the way you look at things, that is wonderful too. There are no rules. There are no boundaries, nothing to hold you back. Only yourself. Only you can create self-inflicted rules and boundaries. You have control of your life. You are in the driver's seat, and you can have whatever you choose to have.

If you choose to sit alone in a room and meditate for twenty-four hours, seven days a week, so be it. If you choose to engage with others and have fun and romp, play, and experience life as children do, that is fine as well. Observe the little children.They are always delighted and living in the moment. They experience life full of joy. Any little thing gets them excited. The children are the teachers. The children have the answers.

You are starting to realize that you have the power, have always had the power to experience life for the joy and the fun of it. So be free to be you. Experience life from a place of wonder. Engage fully in life. As you look at a butterfly, cherish it. See it with all of its beauty and glory and colors and experience that. From this new perspective, be one with it. As it flies away, be with it and sense the ever-expanding universe that is yours for the taking.

We would like to offer an approach that will help you turn negative and unwanted thoughts and experiences into positive thoughts and affirmations. If you are stressed, angry, resentful, sick, injured, depressed, overwhelmed, unhappy, or just feel hopeless, you are most likely giving your power away to another person, place, thing, or illness. You may be caught up in a habitual negative or resistant attitude or response to life events. All of these things are the result of powerlessness and not living and being your whole self. You unconsciously forgot who you really are.

That which we call The Turn-Around Solution are processes to reclaim your power. If you will take the time to be still and experiment with our suggestions, it will help you to change the way you perceive the challenge, to change your inner perspective, and to gradually regain your power.

1. Be honest with your feelings.

Awareness and honesty are extremely important in transforming your life. Often people are not aware of the beliefs that not only surround their fears, but also create them. Often they blame others or outside circumstances for their misfortunes. Often they are in denial. Therefore, it is important to first identify your feelings and realize that these feelings are only a reflection of a recent or current state of mind, or of a habitual emotional response to an outer circumstance.

It is important to ask yourself what exactly is it that you are feeling, to become aware of your emotions. Usually patterns of fear, anger, and worry are so habitual; they become a way of life. Therefore, after acknowledging whatever emotions you are feeling, the first step is to stabilize those emotions. Tell yourself, "The negative emotions I'm feeling now were created by me, so I can change the way that I feel by changing the way I look at things. I can be more in control in my life by choosing future thoughts and responding to circumstances in a much more positive way."

2. Make peace with yourself and the current situation.

Accept and love yourself unconditionally, and be gentle with yourself. Interact with yourself the way you would with a frightened child. Many people beat themselves up with criticism and condemnation for being in an unfavorable situation. Embrace the person, place, or situation by realizing that in every circumstance you are working within your belief system. The more you judge, criticize, punish, or resent the perceived "perpetrator," or judge or resist the condition, the more those people will push back, or the condition will worsen. It's important to remember that because of the law of attraction, you always attract people or events of a similar vibration.

As you would show compassion to a child, embrace yourself, literally. Hug yourself. Pamper yourself and soothe your emotions by thinking about your favorite things. When you are down, try replacing your negative thoughts and feelings with things that make you feel good. Take a long bubble bath, listen to uplifting music, or go for a walk in nature. Reading and listening to spiritual and self-empowering recordings are always beneficial.

3. Identify the beliefs behind the fear and powerlessness and reclaim your power.

Your world and the entire universe are newly created in each precious powerful moment. Each moment has the potential for new birth, regardless of any past moments. Humans do not realize how powerful each moment is. Know now that you can replace any negative belief or emotion with one that is positive and life affirming. Listen to your self-talk and observe your habitual emotional responses to people or circumstances that leave you feeling negative or fearful. Become more aware of your continual patterns of resistance, defensiveness, and negative expectation.

Beliefs and habits are reinforced from moment to moment, and from day to day, and are even passed on to offspring from generation to generation. All negative reactions are a reflection of individual, personal, societal, or collective erroneous beliefs. Therefore, negative emotions can assist you in identifying an erroneous belief. If you don't feel good, you're seeing something from a limiting perspective and not from a higher perspective based on natural, universal laws.

Review the natural universal laws we have talked about. You may believe these universal laws intellectually, however, because of all the years of conditioning, you do not believe them on a visceral or vibrational level. If you did, your life would not be producing adverse experiences. Your emotional responses have become so habitual that they are actually a part of your cellular and neurological biology.

4. Affirm that you live in a safe universe.

We cannot emphasize enough that any lasting change must be implemented moment by moment. Consistently ask yourself, "How does this feel?" If you don't feel good, deliberately choose a thought that creates a more positive feeling and positive expectancy. Know in each moment that life is always for you. Know that your universe can be safe, abundant, harmonious, joyful, and full of health and vitality. Know that the universe is conspiring to bring you prosperous, fulfilling opportunities.

Know viscerally that the infinite, powerful force of All That Is is the inspiring essence within every atom, molecule, plant, creature, and human. Know that you live in an abundant universe, that you are worthy and deserving, and that prosperity is your rightful inheritance. The belief in scarcity is the main cause of so much pain and suffering for people and nations. Remember that the law of attraction that can bring unfavorable experiences in your life also has the power to bring you the material things, relationships, and events that make your heart sing. It is important to note, however, that the main reason you desire material things is for the feeling of freedom, joy, peace of mind, and the opportunities and experiences they can offer you.

Any preconceived threat from anything outside of you can only manifest if you concentrate on it or give it energy. Always expect the best. As you remember that you are by divine right a powerful creator and begin to trust and allow the process of life, you will see things turn-around.

5. Change your perceptions, change you vibration

Be aware that your emotions are a natural, universal part of every being. Your emotions are the indicator of your perceptions. The information your emotions give you is your feedback system for what is happening in your life. When you don't feel good or are experiencing negative emotion, life is letting you know that you aren't seeing something from your highest perspective.

Becoming more aware of your emotions and responses is all part of knowing of self. Knowing yourself is the first step in making real and lasting change. Pay attention to those natural indicators and ask yourself, "How can I look at this situation differently? Perhaps I could respond to that in a different way. Perhaps I could talk to that individual with a different attitude." The change must come from within you.

You are not trying to correct anything on the outside, but are using outer circumstances and emotions as a mirror to reflect your limiting perceptions. With that understanding, you can begin to see for yourself and gain new perceptions. Changing your inner attitudes will change the outer experiences. Once you look at the undesired situation from the point of power, you automatically transform your vibrational frequency. Consequently, through the law of attraction, you will draw to you a different outcome. You get what you concentrate on.

6. Imagine your preferred outcome.

Imagine the preferred outcome to your challenge or crisis. In doing this, it is best to focus less on specifics, and more on how it feels to have the problem resolved for the highest good of all concerned. Often you limit the preferred intent by being too attached to a specific result. Sometimes it is better to allow the universe to manage the particulars.

The most important aspect of this process is to become a vibrational match to whatever it is you desire. You are not a vibrational match when you are worried about how something will be resolved, or when you are feeling negative emotions from erroneous beliefs about yourself, others, or the situation.

You may also want to record affirmations and other inspirational messages on a tape or disc and listen to them before you go to sleep, or when you get up, or throughout the day. Or sounds of nature. Or uplifting music.

And most importantly, say to yourself, "All is well in my world and, when I get out of my own way, I live a life of abundance and joy and satisfaction." Remember the power of being alive. Remind yourself to take a moment to clear your mind and shake off the resistance and fear. Bring yourself back into your loving and powerful Source Self. Remember that the point of power is the point of peace, that your power comes from within. Choose life. Breathe. Feel life filling you up and embracing you. Feel life take you by the hand and lead you along the path to empowerment, back to your whole, soul self. Feel your non-physical, physical, and ego self cooperating in harmony with All That Is.

CHAPTER 9
Healing: Whatever Works

Modern practitioners look down upon what one would call "primitive" medicine. Many primitive cultures had medicine men whose beliefs and treatments varied from culture to culture. Some, for example, believed that those with physical, mental, or emotional illness were cursed with evil spirits that had to be cast out.

Myth, legend, and folklore speak of witch doctors, medicine men, shamans, sorcerers, and priests who performed various rituals and ceremonies to heal someone. These rituals depended on tribal beliefs and included special chants, ceremonial music, dance, and processions. There were magic charms and spells, exorcisms, and even animal and human sacrifices. There are stories of tribes whose witch doctors would sacrifice a chicken during a ceremonial ritual, then place the dead chicken around their neck.

Some of these witch doctors were extremely charismatic and hypnotic and would put a patient in a trance-like state. Some rituals acted as shock treatments that startled and distracted the patients from their painful or stressful experience to the point that it enabled them to focus in the moment. You might say it forced them out of mental, emotional, and physical resistance.

These methods were effective because of the power of the practitioner, and the patient's belief in the treatment. These medicine men or witch doctors in a way hypnotized the individual into releasing the belief that created the malady and replacing it with a new healing and hopeful belief.

Native Americans had a deep connection with the earth and would often use natural herbs and plants to assist individuals in their healing. They would apply poultices to wounds along with chants. The individual who was familiar and accepting of this healing process would respond favorably.

Many individuals today seek particular tools outside of themselves to assist them in feeling safe or in healing themselves or someone else. Often one will seek out someone who performs an alternative healing modality— Healing Touch, Reiki, Body Talk. There are a variety of healing modalities at this point. There will be many more developed in the future.

All healing, however, ultimately comes from within and you can tune into your own natural healing abilities by becoming intuitively aware of how the body works. Your body is a fine machine that will function very well until something pulls it out of balance. Most in western society turn to a physician who will diagnose the symptom and recommend a pill or a injection or further tests to find the imbalance. Generally, neither the physician nor the patient understands that the healing comes from within.

When you are aware that something is not right within your body—you may suffer from frequent headaches or body aches, for example—it is a signal that something is out of balance in some way. Listen to your inner voice and to particular signals when you do not feel well, and know that your body is capable of healing itself. You must understand your beliefs and how you substantiate your beliefs. Understand yourself and know that you can indeed take charge of your own body.

If, however, you feel that a practitioner outside of the self is timely and appropriate for you, we suggest you look at that treatment as a bridge you will eventually cross as you learn to rely more on your own inner healing power. Meanwhile, allow yourself the freedom to choose. Allow things to unfold naturally, without fear or doubt. You can move forward by telling yourself, "I am making this decision because it feels the most appropriate for me at this time." Relax, enjoy, and be at peace with it. Go with your instinct, for no one is walking in your shoes. No one knows your life as well as you do. There is no right or wrong. Follow your instincts and your impulses. They will not lead you astray. But know that becoming aware of the natural, powerful, joyful, spiritual being that you were created to be is the only lasting remedy for health and vitality.

QUESTIONS AND ANSWERS

Ken: Would you say that people, as they evolve, move away from anything that puts the responsibility and healing power outside of self? There are so many misunderstandings.

Orion: It is not our mission to say to anyone that one can or cannot be attracted to a particular tool that is useful at any time in a person's life. There are a myriad of tools, of practitioners and healing modalities that an individual may be drawn to at any particular time in their life depending upon that individual's point of knowing the self. So when beings are in the process of learning about themselves— learning more about how their body feels, how their body reacts, how their body heals itself—they may be drawn to things outside of themselves. They're drawn because, on some level, they believe it will ultimately assist them in learning more about themselves, and about how healing works. This can be useful.

Each of you are separate individuals who have ideas, thoughts, and beliefs that you must work through within your own belief system. You may be drawn to certain things outside of yourself that you believe will help you when something is not in harmony in your body. You will continue to learn and grow in self-discovery.

Ken: And eventually reclaim your power.

Orion: Indeed. You're attracted to certain avenues outside of the self at certain periods of your life, certain periods of personal evolution. As you evolve, you will discover for yourself that you do have the power, have always had the power.

There is no right or wrong. It just is. What we want is for individuals to begin to question, to say to themselves, "Is this something that I want to continue to believe in? Is this something that perhaps I should look at more closely? Is this something that seems a little bit off kilter to me? Am I following blindly? Am I looking for something outside of myself to tell me how I feel? Perhaps it is time for me to look at this a little differently. Perhaps I have been led blindly and have not discovered who I am or my own self-power or self-worth." The power, the choice, and the freedom to decide are still within the individual.

Ken: I think I understand what you are saying. All paths are okay and beneficial for each individual. Everyone acquiesces to what is most beneficial for them at the time, whether that be a certain healer, religion, practice, etc. We learn through our experiences.

Orion: That is precisely what we are saying.

Linda: Something that was difficult to grasp when I first started to become open to these teachings was the idea of going within. I did not understand what that meant when people said to go within. It seemed a little vague to me. Could you explain that further?

Orion: When someone first said that to you what did you think?

Linda: I guess I wondered if that meant that I should meditate. I did not totally understand that we could feel guidance all the time.

Orion: Yes, as you go through life you may discover that something does not feel right, that something seems a little off kilter. On the other hand, you may start to question something that someone tells you. You may feel a reaction within you. Sometimes your reactions are within your mind and sometimes within your body. Sometimes you react with your self-talk, and you may ask yourself, "What is this person trying to say to me?" It does not ring, it does not sing, it does not feel like a fit. That is going within. It is when you question yourself as well as other individuals. When you question, you discover for yourself what resonates with you or what does not. When you find something that resonates, it feels comfortable to you, and it feels like a fit. That comes from listening to your inner voice, your inner guidance. Listen for those signals. Feel the signals. Hear the signals. Your body will also give you signals.

Linda: Thank you. Then it makes sense that people should also go within for the kind of healing that would work best for them. However, the guidance and answers may be different for different people.

Orion: Yes, that is absolutely so. When individuals are listening to themselves, they will be guided to whatever is best for them, whether it be within themselves or something outside of themselves, like a physician or other practitioner, whatever it may be. They are still listening to their inner guidance, and being directed by their inner self. There is no right or wrong. You are being directed by your beliefs, and your beliefs may not be what everyone else's are. It is highly individual. Again, there is no right or wrong. It just is.

Linda: So you are not only saying that there is no right or wrong, but that it all comes down to beliefs.

Orion: Until individuals can figure out precisely what the beliefs and thoughts are that are causing their imbalances, they will keep using tools outside of themselves to assist them. As individuals look outside of themselves, and get feedback and guidance from other individuals or practitioners, if they examine their beliefs and listen to their inner voice, they will gradually begin to look for the answers within.

Self-discovery is, indeed, what the quest is all about— undoing the layers of what makes you tick, discovering what draws you in one direction or another, and listening both outside of yourself and within. What you will discover by listening to your inner voice is that you are the one in charge of your life. You are the creator. When you finally know that, everything else will unfold naturally.

Ken: So whatever the issue, we need to remind ourselves of the truth of those natural universal laws that we discussed earlier. If we are not seeing things from the higher perspective, we are cutting off or resisting our connection to Source Energy. Essentially, what we need to do is remind ourselves that there is only well-being. Correct?

Orion: Yes, that there is only well-being. That you come from the non-physical into the physical. That there is no separation between the non-physical and the physical, and that you come from pure, positive Source Energy, whatever you choose to call it, and it is all well-being. There is nothing out of whack. It is all perfect, beautiful, loving, harmonious, and peaceful. However, when you are not in harmony with that well-being, you will get the signs and indicators. They will say, "Wake up! This is not right. Something is not right here!" They will bang you on the head saying, "Hello. We are calling you. Listen." Then you remember to tap into that voice within. You tap into that inner guidance. You tap into that energy essence of you. You listen and pay attention to the signals.

Linda: I know you said everything is a belief, but is it possible we could actually create evil entities or evil spirits. For example, some people have been known to create an alter ego or split personality that is real to them even though it is all in their mind. Is this similar to people who believe in evils spirits and possession? Are their creations all in their mind or are they real?

Orion: They are thought forms. A thought is never lost. Some people are more sensitive to thought forms. So if a person who is sensitive walks into a particular house that is considered to be haunted, and moves about from room to room, he may indeed pick up on some energies that are still hanging around. Thought forms are everywhere you go. They are not just in a particular house. You could pick up thought forms or energy in anyone's home, or walking down the street, or in a department store. There are thought forms everywhere.

Ken: Can you comment on vaccinations?

Orion: It has long been one of your societal beliefs that you must guard against outside forces and invaders. From birth, your collective beliefs have affected your cells, organs, and immune systems both consciously, unconsciously, and telepathically. Your body is well equipped to handle anything that, what some may say, can attack or invade your body like certain germs or viruses. As long as you are vulnerable because of these socially-accepted diseases, we would highly recommend you take any vaccinations that you believe will protect you.

Ken: What about smudging, surrounding yourself in white light, and using crystals, and aromatherapy?

Orion: Smudging is a practice that people believe protects them, clears evil or lost spirits, or negative or fearful energy left in a room by others. We assure you that even if there were negative thought forms, nothing can ever harm you from the outside unless you have those beliefs.

Yes, crystals can be great conductors of energy, but you do not need them.

Now, if you would ask Leslie, she would say, "I love aromatherapy." If the scent of flowers, incense, the cooking of baked goods, meat, or whatever uplifts you or makes you feel good, then we say be in the joy of it.

It is mind blowing how may rituals humans have invented to protect, heal or give their power away. In reality, you have always had the power intrinsically all along. Absolutely nothing can harm you without your acquiescence. But, we would rather those with these limiting beliefs perform the smudging or use incense and holy water than remain fearful. Whatever works for you.

However, we want you to know that there is absolutely nothing required to fix, protect, or heal you, because life is good. Only your fears, erroneous beliefs, and not being your authentic, whole, natural self can harm you.

Ken: What about astrology?

Orion: There are cycles, lunar and cosmic influences, and other energies that affect the body because the body is comprised of water, but you always have the ability to thrive despite any outside influence. Everything is composed of energy and there are changing frequencies and intensities. People all have different personality characteristics and tendencies, and if an astrologer can empower you with guidance, then use it. Our message once again is to use whatever tools serve you. Always make the final decision for direction yourself. You are never a victim. Nor are you at the effect of any celestial or astrological phenomenon. Life is always for you.

We had heard so many far out predictions for December 12, 2012 and December 21, 2012. Stories of how suddenly there will be peace on earth and everyone instantly healthy and enlightened. Or how there will be the total collapse of your economic system, how millions of people who do not become enlightened will disappear from the planet.

Or reports that the earth will turn over on its axis. Those days have come and gone without either the catastrophic or miraculous events.

Now from our perspective, yes there were changes, but those changes have been occurring significantly for the last twenty years, and will continue to do so. Yes, there has been an acceleration of energy, therefore whatever you place your attention on will manifest more rapidly than ever before. So within this acceleration, you will feel like events and things in your life are happening more quickly. If you focus your mind and emotions in a positive direction, you shall reap favorable experiences. If you focus in a negative direction, you will experience the undesirable.

Nevertheless, we want to emphasize that there are no victims and no one can evolve in consciousness without their own volition. Everyone evolves at their own pace. There has never been and can never be any coercion or force from anyone or anything outside of each being. Do you or do you not create your reality? The universe and every consciousness therein is eternally expanding.

To summarize, we are not saying that any of the systems above are bad or that you should not utilize them. We are saying to always follow your inner guidance for what is beneficial for you. What is good for one person may not be good for another. Similarly, what is advantageous for an individual during a certain level of spiritual evolution may not be beneficial at a later time. It is when individuals are so caught up in trying to find the answers outside of themselves that things become much more complicated than they need to be. Look for and know that the answers are always within. Rest in the ease and comfort of your own being. Relax and enjoy the peace, love, and harmony of an inner-directed life.

CHAPTER 10

Relationships

When you are in love with self, embracing self, and accepting of yourself unconditionally, that is the best relationship you could ever have. When you love and accept yourself, you are in harmony and find no fault with anyone. This is unconditional love. If someone irritates you, it is because of something within yourself that has been generated outward. The instigating individual is merely a mirror of the irritation within you at that particular time.

Many people in your culture mistake neediness for love. It is something that begins, it seems, with the inception of one's birth, when the child becomes reliant on the mother. There is a special bond between mother and child, and one that helps the infant feel loved. As the child grows, it begins to have its own ideas and beliefs. Often these are discouraged or even disallowed. Without the nurture of individual expression, children may become in need of outside validation. When boundaries are put upon children expressing themselves freely, openly, and honestly, they become less of themselves. This need for outside validation grows to include not only parents, but siblings, teachers, and peers.

As they grow, these children come to accept the boundaries set upon them, and become less of an individual and more of a pleaser, for that is a way they find outside validation they crave. As they mature, they begin to experiment with intimate relationships. Often they find themselves trying to please the object of their affection so he or she will love them in return. This is the beginning of conditional love in relationship. This is when they find themselves saying things like, "I will love you if... I will love you because... I will love you when..." All of those things add up to an unhealthy relationship. They are denying themselves and the other the freedom to express in an authentic way.

It is very important that each being be free to express who they came forth to be. Encourage your children to be true to themselves and to believe in themselves. Try not to push upon them what you expect from them or want them to be. They come into this life with past soul expressions and experiences that make them who they are now. Your children are here to express themselves.

When you are inner-directed or self-directed, you are not in need of conditions or of anyone else's approval. When you are self-directed and inner-directed, there is not need for outside validation, for you are free to express yourself openly and honestly without boundaries.

When you are in love with yourself, you give yourself the permission to love and accept yourself just as you are. You will then draw to you others that have this same clear sense of self. You will choose to be together because you enjoy being together, not out of need.

When you find yourself in a relationship, whether it is a love relationship or a work relationship, and you feel in harmony with an aspect of another, that, too, is reflecting a part of you. When relationships do not outwardly appear to be going as you would wish, take time to reflect. The answer is within you. Perhaps you find yourself being angry at inappropriate times or frustrated. Perhaps your intimate partner and you no longer seem to agree on things the way you did when you first came together. This is, in part, because you are continually growing and expanding beings.

Step back and observe. You will find that one or both of you are changing, growing, and seeing life from different perspectives. There is nothing wrong with that. You are finding life to be ever-expanding, ever becoming more. Know that in any relationship there is always growth and expansion. So enjoy the process and know that there is no right or wrong about it.

When you find friction in any kind of relationship, know that at the root is something within you that you are wanting to find out more about, some part of yourself to explore, something about yourself to discover. Relationships are about the self first. When you realize this, all relationships will become less tense, less frightening. It is what it is, and you are learning to love and accept it for what it is.

You are the most important person in your life. When you love yourself and accept yourself, you can look into the mirror and admire yourself, truly look and find all the wonderful qualities that you have and appreciate all of them. You appreciate your face, hair, eyes, nose, and mouth. Your miraculous internal organs, which continually perform without you even thinking about them. You know that you are a beautiful being of light, love, harmony, peace, beauty, joy, and fulfillment. You are truly in touch with the wondrous soul that you are.

You indeed can appreciate you as you are regardless of how others may see or speak of you. You see only the good about yourself and appreciate everything regardless of outer appearance. To you, outer appearance makes no difference. What is most importance is your inner being, and that inner being is where all the love is. Therefore, when you love, accept, and appreciate self, you generate love from your inner being outward. It exudes from every pore of your being, and others will find you just as beautiful and loving as you find yourself.

When you are inner-directed and know your true self and believe in yourself, you relate to others more easily. Relationships with your boss, your family members, your friends, your loved ones fall into place quite naturally. Sometimes, however, relating with a mate can seem more challenging because there are two personalities involved. You may feel as though your rightness is being infringed upon. You must remember you are two separate, whole entities that have your own likes and dislikes, and allow one another the freedom to express as each of you chooses.

We want to stress that it is important for each of you to remain true to the self and to respect that in each other, especially in situations when each partner believes that his or her way is the right way. Take a moment to bring yourself back to center, to remember that even as you are part of the whole of this relationship, you are individuals who must follow your own inner guidance.

QUESTIONS AND ANSWERS

Ken: Can you talk about those who have children because that is what they feel they are meant to do?

Linda: Also about people who seem to have children to fill a void in their lives or to have something on the outside love them? Please address the empty nest syndrome, how when their grown children leave, they feel they have nothing because they gave their power away to their children.

Orion: Yes. We will remind individuals that parenting is an important aspect of one's livelihood. In the case of perhaps a teenager deciding to bring forth a child, it is often a decision made in a moment of lust, rather than of love. Often these teenagers and their babies become an extended family of their parents and grandparents. They often think that having this child will be an extension of love, but what they find is more responsibility than they had ever anticipated. When the responsibility is right there in front of them, they often begin to question their decision. They sometimes find that they cannot even be responsible for themselves. In many cases, their own mothers or grandmothers take on the responsibilities of raising the new child.

These young teenage mothers have been looking for love outside of themselves, rather than finding that love within. They have looked for something they believed would give them that love. In this situation, however, they often realize they have taken on more than they thought they could handle. They come to realize that they now have this other human being that they're responsible for, and yet they do not know how to love themselves. They are looking for love from other beings without knowing that the love they seek is already within them. Only when you love yourself first can you truly share love with another being.

Some parents take on the role of parenting and they have fun with it. They feel the joy of it and they have all of these wonderful adventures that accompany it. Others bring forth children because they are looking for love outside of themselves. They think that children will fulfill the void they feel within, that children are what brings love.

In the case of empty nest syndrome, the understanding that love comes from within, not from any other, even one's children, is missing. Therefore, when the children leave the nest, the parents feel that the love, too, has flown. It is time for them to step back and realize that their children were not meant to fill that void, that what was missing has always been within themselves, and it is something they can reclaim at any time. Future generations will be more conscious and aware in making the decisions regarding whether or not to have children and how many.

Ken: There are so many people that seem to put their lives on hold looking for Mr. and Ms. Right, especially young people right out of high school or college. They place so much emphasis on outer appearances instead of the inner characteristics. Can you talk about two whole people that are healthy and self-fulfilled that just want to share their lives?

Orion: Yes, the best way to attract a healthy relationship is to first be healthy yourself. To discover on your own that the love connection begins with you, with knowing who you are and knowing that you are a powerful being. It is when you are looking for something outside of yourself that you have given your power away. That's where the disconnection begins. When you reclaim that power, you are true to yourself, and you love yourself, you mirror this outward.

This connection to All That Is is never broken, unless you break it. When you break it, you have given your power away. Until you get back to center, back to whole, back to the power within, you will have broken relationships, relationships that are not healthy, relationships in turmoil. So we suggest that you start looking for love first within. Find that powerful connection back to who you are, that love connection to yourself. When you do, you realize that you can see love anywhere—in the grocery, the bookstore, walking down the street. You look at someone and smile and think, *Ummmm, there is a nice love connection.* Love is reflected back to you by everything outside of yourself.

Ken: And as far as people dating and having relationships, you have talked about making it fun, making it a journey, an adventure, and not worrying about whether or not it's going to last, or be "the one." Can you talk a little more about that?

Orion: Yes, do not be so serious about it all. Enjoy it. Have fun. If you are looking for love in all the wrong places—from the exterior rather than the interior sources—you will find that you will often be disappointed. You may have found an individual with the right bone structure, the right eye color, the right hair color, the right height, weight and all of the other externals, but what is missing is the connection to self, their connection to their love of self. If you continually look for something on the outside rather than the inside, you will continue to have relationships that feel off kilter.

We tell you, however, to have fun with whatever you are looking for, and to remind yourselves that by loving self first, and being true to self, and being connected to the powerful self you are, you will discover many individuals that will want to be in your love circle. Your love circle will have a variety of people, many kinds of personalities, appearances, male and female. So enjoy the journey, and being in this beautiful ride of life. Every experience you have will bring forth a new discovery of self.

Ken: My last question is about the inability to say no. Leslie and I have talked a lot about that in the last couple of weeks. It's so hard for us to say no.

Orion: Yes, indeed that is a very difficult for many people to say no, because it seems to be selfish. You are individuals who are here to please self first. So in any kind relationship, whether work, social, whatever, if you are questioning something that feels off kilter, step back and reflect. Do not say yes to doing things because you do not want to hurt another's feelings. Instead, be true to yourself. Do not do something, and then think, "Why in the world did I just say I would do something that I don't want to do?" When you have said yes to something you wanted to say no to, not only does it feel very uncomfortable, but also sometimes, it can even create disease from the imbalance within you. Know that its okay, it is acceptable to say no, if it is coming from your inner guidance. When you are true to yourself, you are a much happier person.

Linda: Sometimes though, in certain situations, I find I have to compromise. Maybe on the surface I don't want to do something, but down deep I really do because I care about that other person.

Orion: We want you always to ask yourselves if it is really something that you want to do.

Ken: You might ask yourself, "Is this something that I want to compromise on?"

Orion: Precisely.

Linda: We have talked about how relationships are changing and partnerships are changing. Do you see marriage as a healthy institution and one that will remain? Do you still see a need for marriage?

Orion: We would not say that there is no need for marriage, only because there are still societal norms, certain rules and regulations, and the institutions of religion. We see that there is definitely a shift whereby individuals are now believing that they can co-habit with another human being without having to have a contract, without having to sign a piece a paper saying that they will love and be together for ever and ever. In reality, who in the world could ever make such a promise to anyone?

These are things you should all decide for yourselves. "I will be with this person because I want to be with them. I don't have to be with them. I don't need to be with them. I choose to be with them. I enjoy my relationship with this person." You do not need something outside of yourself— a signed piece of paper, or 300 witnesses sitting inside of a church. You are all here to enjoy yourselves, to be who you are, and free to choose who you want to be with in joy. If the joy is no longer there, then why would you remain in such a relationship? Therefore, we would say that there is definitely a shift, there are definitely more individuals that are questioning old ideals, but the institution of marriage will remain for now.

Linda: Would you talk about homosexuals parenting children, because that's becoming more prevalent now?

Orion: Yes. This is all going to remain controversial, because individuals in society are not accepting of things they label as abnormal. What we want to stress is that there is nothing abnormal about being with someone that you enjoy being with, someone that you feel a love connection with, whether it be two males or two females. It does not matter. It only matters to those that are pointing their fingers, condemning, and making judgments. There is no ultimate judgment. When you love yourselves, it really matters not who or what sex the person you are in relationship with is. It really matters not. If you are enjoying the relationship, truly enjoying it, and you are in love with each other, you are expressions of that love. If you want to bring a child into that love, so be it. It is all a natural part of the love circle. Even if you have a surrogate to bring forth this being, that person and that child are coming into this love circle through the connection you all share. They have chosen you, just as you have chosen them.

If, however, you believe in societal rules and regulations, then we suggest that you continue in that mode. We say, be true to yourself. Nevertheless, know that you do not have to be ruled by boundaries outside of yourself. Either way, you are here to enjoy life and to be the expression of who you are.

Linda: Can you share a little about how other cultures that do not have the kind of family structure we do experience relationships?

Orion: Yes, they just have an understanding, you see. It sometimes is even a silent understanding. It is something that has transpired between individuals that have this knowing that they are together because they choose to be together. They have this knowing that they are expressions of life, that they are enjoying life, that they are loving what is. They are being true to themselves. That is the grandest expression of love.

In some tribal cultures, one woman may have twenty-five men, or one man may have seventy-five women, and it does not matter. They are all in acceptance. They are all in knowing that that is how it is. There is no competition.

Linda: It is amazing to me how we have distorted love through our neediness. We believe if your mate even looks at another man or woman, it means they do not love you any more.

Orion: Yes. We want you to realize that when you are expressing yourselves and you are true to yourselves and when you know yourselves, most importantly when you love yourself, you can indeed have exchanges of love with a myriad of people in your life. The most important thing to remember is to love self first, to know that you have a divine connection to All That Is.

When you are loving of self first, you will not *need* someone else to be in your life. You will not *need* anything except the love of self. When you have that, you exude it from every pore of your being. When your love shines, people are drawn to you. Although there is absolutely no need, there may be a desire for someone with whom to express that love, to perhaps share your life with. So love yourself, be true to yourself, and enjoy yourself.

Ken: What's the most important thing we need to know about sexuality?

Orion: Know that you are sexual beings. Do not be afraid to openly express yourselves regarding sexuality in any way. It is your natural state of well-being to express sexual desire. Society, church, family have all dictated how you should or should not behave sexually. We want to tell you to be yourselves, free yourselves from all of those boundaries and open yourselves up to expressing what feels good to you. If you don't find a need to be sexually expressive, so be it. Be true to self by all means. That is our message, be true to self.

Chapter 11

The Language of Health and Illness

Why is it some people are the epitome of health and wellness and others are sickly? You choose health and wellness, ease of life or dis-ease. It is your choice. You can choose to listen to those old tapes from parents or the medical community warning you of things to come, or you can take charge of your life and think of wellness being the rule rather than the exception. You are responsible and only you. So in all of these probabilities and choices and freedom, how do you look at health? Do you look at it from the eyes of others or from your own self-knowing?

During periods of chronic worry or stress, you must discern the cause of the negative emotions and the related thoughts that produce the vibrational dis-ease. Most worry is the fear of an immediate or future loss, pending pain, or struggle in financial, relationship, or health issues. No matter the cause, if there is illness, it is the result of feeling powerless. The first step is non-judgmental awareness. If you notice self-talk such as, "I shouldn't feel this fear." Or "Will I ever learn how to create my reality of choice?" start the turn-around solution by positive self-talk. Say, "At least I'm aware of these thoughts, and unlike times before, I will now try to soothe my fear and recognize what or who is depleting my power."

All disease is a result of either erroneous beliefs about the cause of illness or intense or continued stress that has impeded the natural flow of the body's systems, such as a weakened immune system. Illness is language, and the physical symptoms and their location in the body are usually indicators that will reveal thought and feeling patterns. Your day-to-day life, including your health or illness, is always a mirror of your mental and emotional state and your beliefs.

The following are just a few general examples of symptoms and their underlying associated causes and questions to ask yourself.

Headache: Am I being open to new ideas? Do I trust my instincts? Where am I not being flexible?

Neck pain: Am I being flexible? Am I looking in all directions? Where might I be stuck?

Eyes: Am I having trouble seeing the future, past, the now?

Ears: What is it I don't want to hear?

Throat: Am I expressing myself and being true to myself? Am I able to express my feelings and emotions? Can I speak out for myself and stand up for myself?

Arms: Am I able to embrace life? Can I reach beyond?

Hands: Do I have a handle on things? Am I holding on to things too tightly?

Feet: Am I allowing myself to move in whatever direction feels best to me? Do I feel supported by my own well-being? Am I being flexible?

Back pain: Do I feel support not only from self, but also from others in my life? Are my finances supportive of my lifestyle?

Lungs/Breath: Am I allowing myself to take in life? Do I allow myself to give and to receive, like taking in and releasing of breath?

Heart: Am I allowing joy and love into my life?

Stomach: Am I allowing the digestion and assimilation of new ideas, thoughts, feelings, and emotions to flow through me?

Take your power back by knowing that your body is, by its very nature, a powerful biological machine that is self-regulating without effort or understanding on your part of how it works. So even if the energetic dis-ease becomes manifested in a physical disease, remind yourself that wellness is the natural state, not illness. Recall the way your body felt when you felt at ease in it, when you skipped, jumped, and played, when you were not so serious about life. Recall times when you were comfortable in your body.

The way you respond to circumstances and how you feel about situations has a bearing on health and wellness. You think and feel yourself into disease. You think yourself into feelings of unworthiness, guilt, and the consequent lack of well-being. Through your habitual negative emotional responses, you can manifest disease. You can just as easily change your thoughts into ones that reflect the natural ease and comfort that is always within your eternal being.

Try not to put credence and power in what the medical community or well-intentioned friends or family tell you. For example, it is generally believed by the medical and scientific community that you will have a propensity to certain diseases through your genetic heritage.

We want you to know once again, that you are the creator of your reality. Inherited propensities are only probabilities. Perhaps you grew up listening to your parents telling you to have your blood sugar checked because diabetes runs in your family or other such things. What we want you to realize is that these things may be probabilities, but they do not have to manifest. If you believe these warnings, then they become integrated into your belief system. Why not integrate into your beliefs that you are healthy, you are full of life, you have endless strength and vitality instead? That, too, is a probability. So which do you want? Do you want health, wellness, vitality, and strength? Do you want to be in the mode that attracts the opposite? Again, the choice is yours. This is the law of attraction at work, through your thoughts, your feelings, and your emotions. You are creating all of it.

If you are ill and you are given a diagnosis, the fewer people you tell, the easier it will be for you to turn it around. Telling people tends to reinforce the negative and fearful energy. So if you want people to send you well wishes, reassure them, as you reassure yourself, that all is well in your world, that you are feeling better every day—alive and filled with energy. Sometimes you may have to trick yourself into those thoughts. However, as long as you know your sincere intent and you are true to yourself, you do not stretch the truth too far, you are gradually soothing, and comforting yourself with empowering, self-affirming and life-affirming thoughts, you will find that whatever symptoms or conditions you had will fade away.

Whenever your conscious awareness alert system reveals any energetic illness or its consequential physical manifestations, ask yourself, "What led me off of my path of well-being?" Did you listen to other people and their beliefs, or television commercials that warn about such things as winter flu season, colds, fevers, strep throat going around? You might ask yourself why those illnesses don't happen to everyone? You might explore what beliefs about those things you've accepted into your consciousness. Examine and change those beliefs that are not giving you what you want.

Only you know what is best for you. Always listen first to your inner being, your soul self. When fear pokes out its head, soothe yourself with happy thoughts, and stand tall in knowing you are a part of God, that powerful energy stream of well-being. Remind yourself that nothing outside yourself can harm you, that it's your own resistance to self and life that depletes the life flow. Breathe deeply and relax into the ease and comfort of your own being. Tell yourself, "All is well in my life!"

Cancer is one of the diseases most feared. To receive this diagnosis usually puts an individual into a huge tailspin wherein his thoughts, feelings, emotions, and any previous sense of well-being all go down the tubes. Listening to outer medical authorities can make one feel vulnerable and interfere with clear thinking. Stop and ask yourself, "Does what they're saying make me feel better or worse than I already feel?"

You have to take responsibility for your own well-being. Although it is a quantum leap for most, it is indeed something that can be done in a short period of time. However, most people are not ready to take on the responsibility for their well-being, or accept that the disease has been brought about by their beliefs. Therefore, we want to convey that each of you must listen to your own inner guidance. If going to a physician feels like the path of least resistance, then follow that path. If you resonate with alternative ways of healing, that too can help you. If examining your thought patterns and beliefs feels like the path of least resistance, then so be it. The important thing is to think for yourself, to understand your beliefs and how they work, to trust in your inner guidance.

Stress is a major factor in most people's lives. When individuals become stressed by situations or put a lot of stress on themselves, it does indeed take a toll on the body. Each individual experiences stress differently. What can be stressful for one is not necessarily stressful for another.

When you are under a lot stress, you feel it in your body. Your body speaks to you. Your shoulders may become tight, your breathing labored, your bones may creak more, your eyes may feel strained. Your body is asking for release. So relax. Enjoy. Take some deep breaths. Smile. Gently caress your lovely self and be kind to yourself.

Be in appreciation of friends, family, bosses, and co-workers. Life will not seem as stressful when you take time to find the joy and beauty, rather than concentrating on the ills. Realize that everything in your life responds to how you perceive it to be, how you believe it to be. If you feel life is filled with pain, life will give you painful circumstances. If you believe life is full of wonder and joy, then *that* is what life will give to you.

When you are out of alignment, remember that you create your own experiences. Remember that you live in a safe universe where well-being is the rule and not the exception. Review the universal laws. Feel and become the whole inner and outer spiritual and physical being that you were created to be. Know that life is good, that life is for you. Rejoice in the aliveness of you. Love yourself. You'll be amazed at how your body will respond to kind, gentle, and beautiful thoughts, and peaceful feelings.

We want you all to be aware of choices, choices in thoughts, choices in feelings, and choices in beliefs. From any point in your life, you can make changes. You may have taken on the belief of a disease or the belief you are lacking in some area. Become aware of those beliefs. Evaluate them and make a new choice for yourself. Change your limiting thought patterns. Trust that at any point you can change your beliefs to those of health and wellness. Realize there is nothing but well-being and it is not separate from you.

Choosing, looking at, and re-evaluating your beliefs are all a part of finding out who you are and what you want in your life.

QUESTIONS AND ANSWERS

Linda: You've talked about how we can listen to our body, that a pain can be an indicator that we are out of alignment. How can we use these indicators to understand what we're doing that's causing the physical problems?

Orion: The body, mind, and spirit can all be indicators of when things are unbalanced. The most important aspect of life is knowing the self. Whatever symptom you experience—headache, muscle strain, eyestrain, aching bones—is telling you to relax and enjoy life more. To have more fun rather than put undo stress on yourself. That is what is important.

Ken: You have said that illness is a barometer for when the physical self and the ego self are not working in harmony or balance with the soul self or inner self, when we're not trusting and allowing the process of life in joy. Would you say that almost all of the cells in our body respond to this, that our organs cringe or become uptight to the point of restricting their natural flow?

Orion: Yes indeed. Everything has a reaction. It is when the mind, body, sprit connection is being kinked off. You will find that your cells are responding to the very core of your being.

Ken: Is giving up on our desires another vibrational cause for illness?

Orion: Limiting self, not believing in self, lack of self-esteem, and self worth, these are all major factors in health, happiness and well-being. When you are feeling lack or when you are feeling unworthy or not good enough, you are placing yourself in a powerless state of mind, and everything else in your life responds in kind.

Linda: How much does lifestyle, or eating certain foods, or getting a certain amount of sleep contribute to being healthy?

Orion: Again, it all comes down to one's belief system. If you believe that you need eight hours of sleep, that sugar is bad for you, that broccoli is good for you, or that beef is bad for you, then it is. All of this is self-limiting. You come forth from that pure positive state of well-being. When you find yourselves unbalanced or not in harmony with Source Energy, you limit yourselves. You blame exterior things like not enough sleep, eating too much sugar, or eating too much of the wrong foods, when in reality there is no such thing. Integrate and balance your life from the inside out. Develop a state of constant knowing that you spring from that, which is always well-being. Stop looking for things outside yourself to blame. When you feel disconnected, remind yourself of your internal state of well-being.

Linda: I understand what you're saying, but aren't there some things that are more natural for our bodies than others? Wouldn't the body respond better to more natural foods than artificial things? Can you say that there are at least some benefits to more natural foods?

Orion: No. We cannot say that. It is an individual thing. When an individual finds that eating a certain food makes them feel uncomfortable, there perhaps is something in that food that does not correlate with the chemistry within their body. But it is not saying that it's because this food is or isn't organic, or whole, or grown from a particular tree or plant. What it is saying is to listen to your body.

Ken: Is it true that if you are connected and centered and working from a point of power, and more importantly if you are inner directed, you will most likely not overeat and you will probably gravitate towards more natural foods or towards a balance?

Orion: It is a balancing act indeed. Listen and know your body. You cannot make generalizations. You are an individual who is wise, healthy, remarkable, and unique. Know yourself and be responsible for knowing what feels best by listening to that inner voice and inner guidance. Your body will tell you and naturally gravitate to what is best for you.

Ken: If you don't have rules, judge yourself, or feel guilty, and you feel connected and balanced, then it's okay that you ate a whole pizza, or a whole box of donuts or cookies.

Orion: And a bottle of bourbon and five packs of cigarettes.

Linda: So even though there was a vibrational cause that prompted you to binge, you are not going to suffer the effects of that situation?

Orion: If you remain in that continued state of emotional stress rather than return to a state of balance, it will take a toll. When you do the turn-around solution and you change your thoughts and your response patterns, it will not remain detrimental or harmful.

Ken: Once again, it is important to remind ourselves that there is only well-being and that a state of health is natural. I experienced some scary symptoms recently and for the first time I did not run to the doctor immediately. In the past, I would have. Instead, I worked on integrating into my belief system that well-being is the natural order of things and the symptoms went away.

Orion: Yes, and for many individuals going to the doctor is one of those habitual emotional responses that you make because of your beliefs and the way you have looked at life in the past. You seem to think that things happen to you. When you realize that you are the cause of whatever is happening, you can come into alignment with yourself and change your thought patterns, belief systems, and habitual responses. Choose to see things from your point of power, and because of this new perception and new reality and new way of looking at things, they will change. In addition, it feels so good to know how powerful you are.

Linda: We are often told by modern medicine to seek prevention, to have annual checkups, and to go to the doctor even if we are not feeling bad. Could you address this?

Orion: Yes, we say the best preventative medicine is to prevent going to medicine. We want to state emphatically that each of you has the intrinsic ability to heal yourself. Every cell and organ in your body knows what to do without you even realizing it. When you are in tune with yourself, know yourself, and find that something seems a little off kilter, follow your instincts. If your instincts say, "I need to go to a physician to find out what's wrong," follow that instinct. Your body is this miraculous organism of well-being. Develop total faith, belief and knowing that all is well.

When you go to a physician because you believe that you are going there to prevent something, also realize that physicians are trained to search for what's wrong. Often you give your power over to another to give you what is naturally yours—well-being. Probabilities can change. Beliefs can change. Step back and realize once again you are this being of perfect health and well-being and that all is well in your world.

Linda: For example, I do not want to have an annual mammogram anymore. I use to do this because I heard that women over forty need to have this done, but I do not want to do it anymore. Therefore, if my inner self or instinct is to not have this done, there is no reason to do so just because the medical community tells me to. Is this correct?

Orion: Certainly. Many, many women out there do not go and have mammograms or pelvic exams because they know themselves. They know their body and trust in self. However, if your belief system is such that you feel an impulse to go to the physician, listen to that voice as well.

Linda: Another thing that comes to mind is the whole idea of insurance. I feel on some level it makes people rely on something outside of themselves instead of trusting their body and trusting in their wellness. In a way, they are betting on illness.

Orion: If you believe that you need insurance, we would certainly say to get the insurance. Individuals are giving their power away. They are giving it to someone else. It instills fear and lack of trust in self.

Linda: Why do some individuals come into this life with what society labels as disease—cerebral palsy, mental deficiency, deafness, etc.

Orion: They have chosen for themselves a different lifestyle.

Linda: Do you know how difficult that is for people to hear?

Orion: We do know that. The concept of choosing one's parents, or lifestyle, or sexual orientation, for instance, is a very difficult concept for most people to understand. We are encouraging you to use your imagination. Drop the boundaries and let yourselves imagine. For instance, while you dream, you can feel yourself doing things that you do not normally do in the waking state. When you are dreaming you have no boundaries and you are open to endless possibilities.

When you come into the world, you have endless possibilities to choose from, some may choose a lifestyle of poverty, some one of wealth. Some may choose intellectual challenges; others may choose to be geniuses. You see, you always have choices. The choices will be made from where you are when you decide to come and play on the planet. No one has the right to judge you or anyone else for the choices that are made. There is no judgment from All That Is. They are all choices made by your soul self.

CHAPTER 12
Money and Career

Money is Energy

Life and All That Is is always supporting and resourcing you. Within this universe, you are engaged in constant currents of magnetic energy that is transformed into physical manifestations. There are natural phases and cycles such as the seasons, ocean tides, menstruation, birth, and death. Money is merely an energy that is usually exchanged for gifts, ideas, services, products, etc. Currency represents the flow of money energy. When your physical self is aligned with your inner self, you are living a natural life where your personal physical energy as well as you money currency flows abundantly. Your emotions express your energy in motion, e-motion. Blockage in your physical body, your emotions, or your relationship with self or others will negatively affect the flow of money in and out of your life.

All blockage or diminishment of energy is caused by feelings of powerlessness that arise out of fear, doubt, scarcity beliefs, worthiness issues, or lack of self-confidence. Often people will take classes and do affirmations and visualizations in order to attract the best career, relationships, or money. When an individual takes too much action, struggling to push events, they will often experience negative outcomes.

Each person transmits through their thoughts, intents, expectations, emotions, and beliefs, and will attract experiences that reflect them. If you have fear and doubt behind any intent, desire, or affirmation, you will create resistance that will block, delay, or prevent the flow. Once you are in harmony with the intent, then you are an active partner with your inner self working in tandem with the universal casting studio.

For instance, if you have recently lost your job, or have fear of losing your job, and you focus on the major news stories telling you unemployment is up and more and more people can't find work, you have zoomed in on all the negativity, and you will feel more and more defeated. To counteract that, you must focus on your skills, talents, and the ability to thrive and fulfill your dreams and create the reality of choice. Always remember that your words should match your inner being. Your inner being is always saying, "Everything works out for me. Abundance is my natural inheritance, and I am always worthy of the best."

Once you have clear intentions that do not contain fear, doubt, and scarcity, hopeful signs will begin to appear in your day-to-day life. Only then will you be ready to take deliberate action. You must be an active participant believing, trusting, and feeling that the universe is a powerful stream of well-being and abundance.

When you are working on your beliefs, often you become mixed up and twisted around, and your thinking gets so convoluted you do not know which direction to go in. Often you are more motivated by negative emotions, and these negative emotions may interfere with the natural flow of prosperity. Prosperity is more a feeling than an intellectual thing. Don't continually question whether you should sit back and do nothing or take action. Relax and know that this is an abundant universe. When you come from that knowing, that authentic self, you will know when to wait and when to act in a timely and appropriate way. You will manifest your abundance naturally. Maintain clear intentions and appropriate actions and your universal casting studio managers will direct those search beams out to your day-to-day world where they will scan for beneficial opportunities.

Become a conscious creator instead of just responding to events and circumstances. When you observe the relationship between your thoughts, feelings, and emotional responses, and what plays out in your life, you understand your power to create. Open up a clear channel of awareness and communication between your inner self and ego self and observe the subsequent synchronicities and events that unfold. Once you learn to follow the inner guidance, you will know when and what decisions, directions, or actions to pursue.

Casting a Job or Career

Here is an example of how this might work with regard to a job or career. The first thing is to examine your passion and think of a job that would make your heart sing. The passion can be incorporated into whatever is the end result. Understand that you may not be able to get all the way there in one fell swoop. There may be spaces in between, places where you have to make changes, take action, scan for problems and potential solutions. You can attract the essence of anything that you want, but there are usually stepping-stones to get there. Know your strengths and weakness, self-imposed or physically imposed limitations, and time preferences.

Then watch for results.

The evidence is usually right in front of you. Perhaps you receive a telephone call from an acquaintance about someone in need of something you have to offer, and you know it is the result of the intention you sent out. Your casting studio managers are at work for you. Probabilities are at hand—investors, opportunities. Your casting studio managers are collaborating with other agents representing you for potential win-win manifestations.

What if you are shy or doubt your qualifications to take the action and follow up on those leads, or you have second thoughts? What if you miss the first opportunity, or change your intentions and desires? The casting mangers will say to your personal agents *let's send e-mails, faxes to other agents looking for such and such,* and then more signals and signs in the form of telephone calls or mail come to you seemingly out of the blue.

A situation like this happened to Leslie. She was working at a lab for many years and the company had been bought out several times. During one of these transition times, she sent out several resumes. There was no pressure, fear, doubt, or concern, because to her knowledge, her job was not in jeopardy, and she loved her job and her co-workers. Then suddenly without notice, she was informed she would be losing her job. However, since she had sent out her intention for something new when she had no worries, her casting studio had already been arranging various opportunities that were an electromagnetic match to her beliefs and desires.

One day she received a call from someone that said that although she may not be looking for a job, they have an opening and were wondering if she would be interested. Her response was positive and an interview was arranged. Then more surprisingly, she received a call from someone that interviewed her for a job ten years earlier. She was being sent many opportunities.

When you are in tune with your life, desires, and impulses, your inner casting agent is busy arranging things.

There are invisible forces always working out the details for you. Use your imagination to see and feel whatever it is you desire. If it is a new car, go to a dealership and drive the car of your dreams, or rent that car. If you cannot afford, right now, an expensive meal at a five star restaurant, go there, have a drink, and soak up the ambiance. Feel the wealth, the warmth, and the spirit of the place you wish to dine in. Speak and feel as if you already have the lifestyle you desire. Prosperity is a feeling phenomenon.

Perhaps you went on an interview with the feeling that the job is yours. Two days later, you get a call, and they have chosen someone else. Don't immediately ask yourself what went wrong. There may be something much more appropriate waiting for you. More money, better hours, better benefits, the job that you had dreamt of all your life. Life always attempts to bring you the best.

If you did not get the job, see the positive aspects of the process. "I had a great interview. I got over the butterflies. I was able to talk intelligently about myself and review how good I felt after the interview." Take the good feelings with you and that will help to attract more signs and signals on the way to what you want. It is a process. As you change, the momentum gets you motivated and the picture becomes clearer. The seeds are planted and the sprouting begins. Sometimes cues are missed or misread, but do not be discouraged. Allow the process of life, go with the flow, and do not become hung up on the details. Rejoice in what you have been able to manifest.

Leslie and Ken have done much traveling over their years together. In the beginning stages of their relationship, they had meager salaries, to say the least. However, it was still important to them to travel. In the beginning, it would be small local trips, or short trips.

Then it became out-of-state trips, then trips to other countries. It was done in increments as they grew and understood how to manifest what they desired. Their expanding consciousness and awareness has allowed them to increase their travels to three or four trips per year.

Just like exercise, you do not start out at the top intensive level if you have not exercised in twenty years. You start where you believe you would feel the most comfortable. As you continue with your program, and it gets easier and easier, you move to more intense workouts. You can see the progress, you can feel it in your body, in your well-being. Sometimes you do not even realize how far you've progressed.

QUESTIONS AND ANSWERS

Linda: It's hard to understand that there is only a stream of well-being, or that life is really for us when we see so much pain and suffering on the planet. Can you please elaborate on that?

Orion: When concentrating on pain and suffering, that will be what will manifest in your life. If you are concentrating on what you are wanting, what you are desiring, that is what you will bring to your life. So again, be aware of your responses to life. Be aware of your reactions. Be aware of what it is that you want to bring into your reality. If you desire peace, love and harmony, would you concentrate on war, hatred, and fear? Of course not. Look at things differently. See life as you want it to be. Observe how you react. If you are reacting in a negative, fearful, or hurtful way, you will bring that into your existence. It is a matter of how you think and feel, and how aware you are of your responses.

Linda: What is Prosperity?

Orion: It is not only money, but health, well-being, and love of self. Most importantly, it is being true to self, appreciating and enjoying who you are and what you have whether it is relationships, possessions, or money. Enjoy everything in your life, and live and love freely as the authentic you. To be engaged in the harmonious dance of life, that is prosperity. To be happy, healthy, vital, joy-filled, and loving is prosperity. Prosperity is your rightful inheritance and natural state of life. It is the unconditional love and acceptance and embracing of all the positive and negative aspects of one's experiences.

Ken: What is abundance?

Orion: It is having the time, resources and energy to attract everything you need to satisfy your physical, emotional, and spiritual desires and comfort. When you and Leslie were traveling in Thailand, you saw the smiling faces and joy within the people there, even though you looked at their circumstances and wondered how they could be so happy with what appeared to be so little. Abundance is in how you respond, appreciate, and bring joy into your life by living it fully, completely as you.

Ken: What is Money?

Orion: What is another word for money? Currency. Money is only the practical symbol and exchange system for resources, materials, and services of value. Money is the physical supply, or you may say the visual currency, of the natural currents of life's inexhaustible energy. There is a natural rhythm to money consisting of ebbs and flows and cycles, just like nature's cycles of the moon, seasons, and ocean tides. Humans think that money is limited, so you have manifested an economic system that appears to be finite. We are here to tell you that the universe wants you to manifest all of your desires. Consciousness always seeks to enjoy the transformation of the formless into physical expression and experience through the wonderment of the imagination.

Linda: How can we attract more abundance?

Orion: You are all broadcasting your desire by the thoughts, beliefs, and expectations you emit moment to moment. You will attract the essence of all of your desires, but fear, doubt, and unworthiness will all deter, hinder, limit, or impede their manifestation. You want to act or feel like you already have what you desire. You want to have an invincible knowing and unwavering trust that you inner casting studio has already arranged the responses to your requests. Practice directing your thoughts, fostering a more confident expectancy. Practice enhancing and energizing your intrinsic creativity and imagination. Know that you are worthy of the best and act accordingly.

Ken: Why is scarcity so prevalent in our society?

Orion: It is the belief in scarcity that creates poverty, disharmonious relationships, disease, wars, crime, anxiety, and a need to control your environment. People listen to the doom and gloom on the news, in the marketplace or workplace, and at times it emotionally and physically depletes their energy and resources. Spend more time instead being inner directed, focusing on the abundance of All That Is.

Linda: How can we overcome this belief in scarcity?

Orion: Become more aware of the abundance in nature. Know that by being alive you are worthy and that life always provides everything you need. Tap into and utilize your imagination. Through self-discovery and exploration find your passion, and then use your gifts of imagination to see your life and dreams unfold the way you want them to. Develop a new worldview of people cooperating, thriving, despite what you hear from news and other outside sources. Picture everyone being cooperative. Feel the wealth, health, and happiness, and choose to live life in a way that makes you thrive. Once you trust, allow, and become authentically prosperous, you will be a conscious creator and not a fearful or greedy competitor. Competition has come from a society that does not trust and allow the process of life, nor know how to be in joy. Cooperation is the natural order of the universe.

Linda: What is a beneficial way for a person who has lost his job to go about finding another, or for someone to pursue a new career?

Orion: By understanding oneself. By looking within and peeling away the layers of self. Sometimes it is a trial and error process. Imagine what would make you feel alive, fulfilled, satisfied, and content. Talk about your creative ideas, passions, and strengths. Look throughout your history and emulate people whose passions became reality, especially those who may have been either laughed at or knocked down time after time until they realized their dreams. Know that if you did not have the ability to achieve your visions, you would not have had the fervent desire for them. It is always about trusting and allowing the process of life. When you enjoy the process, life will manage all the details, and you will live your visions as they arise. When you see synchronicity all around you, you will know you are being true to self, and all the resources, opportunities, and people needed will effortlessly fall into place.

Stay focused, confident, inner directed instead of trying to force things to happen. Act upon your impulses and if you are unsure or confused, wait until you are feeling confident about your intent and strategy, then take the necessary action.

CHAPTER 13

Death: Transition and New Adventure

Most people think you are dead *or* alive, non-physical *or* physical. They do not realize that you are both at the same time. You are simultaneously alive *and* dead, non-physical *and* physical. You identify mostly with your physical vehicle and personality, but there is so much more that encompasses your soul self. Most people think of the non-physical as only the death experience. In actuality, even when you are awake, you have an inner self, a much larger part of you that is not in a time-space reality.

Death can be looked at as a transition—the process of changing from one state to another. The death experience is the transitioning from the physical to the non-physical. When you die, however, you take your beliefs with you. If you believe in a heaven and hell and purgatory, you will experience this in the initial phase of the transition. This experience, however, where individuals meet with the out-picturing of their fears and beliefs in judgment will be like having a nightmare in the sense that it will be only a temporary flicker, and for some individuals non-existent.

Your inner being or higher self in collaboration with your other guides and teachers will be there to assist in the initial phase of your transition. When you actually go on to merge your physical self with your soul self, this journey will become an enhanced, surprising adventure, and you will experience a peace, joy, and love that is difficult to describe in words. You will not know these emotions in the same way that they are known to you in the physical, but it will be an experience that will be fulfilling in so many ways. There will be a knowing. You will know that this has happened before, and it will happen again. It will feel like déjà vu. So realize that there is nothing to fear in death, but only a new adventure to look forward to.

What of your life in relation to death? How do you live your life now? Do you come at it feeling that you are only here for a short time, worrying if you can get it all done, fearing what is next? Do you come at it with the knowing that all is well? Live your life in joy, being here and now in the present moment, worrying not about the future or past. If you are concerned about how long you will be here on the earth plane or worrying about what loved ones will do when you're gone, you are cutting yourself off from that ever-flowing stream of life. Look at life from the perspective of loving each and every moment, of living every experience from the point of power that is now.

We want you all to realize that you have had many lifetimes in your soul's experience, but the one you are living now, who you are now, is what is most important. What are your dreams, wishes, and desires now? Be present in this moment. Engage with the flow of life and experience it from the perspective of joy. Know that there is nothing to fear in death.

QUESTIONS AND ANSWERS

Linda: Once we pass through our beliefs after death, do we always enter the natural state of well-being? Is the non-physical always a state of well-being?

Orion: The non-physical is indeed always well-being.

Linda: Is there different awareness beyond beliefs? If when we die, we pass through our beliefs and get back to our true self or natural self, would we be all knowing? Aren't our beliefs what are limiting?

Orion: When you die you don't necessarily become all knowing, because as much as any one person or entity knows, there is that much more that can be learned, realized, actualized, experienced. You drop all doubt, resistance, and fear, and you become one with All That Is. The word "knowing," however, is a relative term to each person or its overall entity self.

All conscious experiences, realizations, insights, and spiritual awareness expand not only the individual, but also the collective awareness of the oversoul or entity self. Therefore, you may say that any conscious spiritual realizations, awareness, and expansion are an eternal investment. Each person and his or her overall entity are on a different spiritual evolutionary path. Any unfulfilled desires from one life can be evaluated during the after death experience, and those unmet desires can either be played out with probable selves or future reincarnation selves.

CHAPTER 14

Living in the God Zone

How does one understand the true nature of the soul self when there have been so many words for soul, God, and the ego? Words can never adequately describe the many aspects of God, which include all aspects of the universe, including your inner soul self integrated with your outer physical self. Although ultimately everything is all one, within that collective beingness are billions of individualized entities. Within each entity are soul selves that include personality egos that all have the freedom to create, express, and explore their unique choices.

We prefer to use *All That Is* to express God because humans have so many misconceptions about and man-made concepts of what the word "God" means. Nevertheless, for purposes of this book we will continue to use the term God, since the majority of people on the planet are more comfortable with it. Trusting and allowing the process of life cannot be achieved by intellectual knowledge alone, but must be an emotional feeling, an inner believing and knowing. Your visceral realization and awareness of the nature of God and the partnership of the physical and non-physical is the prerequisite to this trust and allowance. God is the total gestalt collective and culmination as well as the source of everything in all universes. God is ultimate integrity.

There is no place where God is not. The relationship between the non-physical inner self and the physical self, which includes your personality and ego self, is a divine partnership. They are not separate, but always parts of a cooperative, interactive, and interconnected whole self. When you, as a physically focused personality, recognize this, then you interact with this responsive inner identity and become a conscious, active member of what we call your "super soulful dream team."

The more you practice this interactive dynamic partnership and utilize your powerful inner self, the more you will radiate peace and joy to the outer world. When this happens, you could say that you have entered The God Zone. Living from The God Zone means loving self first, and accepting everything and everyone without conditions or boundaries. It means becoming consciously aware of your own capabilities and how you want to experience your life. To not being concerned about how others want to live their lives. It means co-existing peacefully with all humans, animals, and nature.

The God connection is the ultimate, divine relationship that you so desired as you chose to become physical in this and every lifetime. It is difficult to express in words the all-encompassing love that is eternally showering you from your inner soul self. This boundless unconditional love and acceptance is always beckoning for your conscious awareness, but because of fear, self-denial, and self-doubt you unconsciously ignore its presence.

Humans have allowed their ego selves to dominate them and their cultures, thereby denying their greater inner self. We are not dismissing the ego or saying or implying it is inferior. We do not want you to either. It is an important part of your earthly personality. When you judge, belittle, or criticize ego, you demean yourself. Most people in you world identify themselves as their ego personality, so to discount ego is to deny the unique and precious identity self that expresses aspects of your greater being.

We do, however, see that currently your ego identity is out of balance. It is when you balance that ego self and align with your inner self that you overcome the belief in your own powerlessness and recognize and feel your own validity and worth. Everyone and everything is worthy. It is your birthright. When you cultivate the balance, you will no longer need outside validation, but own the creativity, power, and joy that are inherently yours.

What does it mean to be a conscious creator? How do you remain centered in a world that is swirling around you? How do you find the peacefulness during unmerciful times? You may find yourself listening to the news or having an intense conversation with someone, and suddenly you become entwined in a mix of emotions and activity. Leslie had a day at work when an irate customer called spewing harsh words and innuendos at her. Afterwards, she felt depleted, shaken from her previous feeling of peace.

These kinds of scenarios happen on a daily basis. So what can you do? You can reassure yourself that it was simply a moment, a temporary state, where you have allowed yourself to be pulled off center. You can remind yourself that if you wallow in what happened on the outside, you only make it more difficult to return to your inner well-being. Moreover, when you are off-center, life will give you things to look at and examine that show you how off-center you are.

Instead, remind yourself that you don't have to be at the effect of what happened. You can regain your center, your balance. Breathe. Relax. Listen to some music, if you can.

Don't get stuck in the muck and the mire, but allow yourself to have the experience, to reflect on it, learn from it, see why it happened, and choose to get back into the zone. When you are back in the zone of happiness and joyfulness, you will have those ah-ha moments. You will stand in a grocery line and someone will say, "You only have a few items please step in front of me." You will have people wanting to go out of there way to assist you.

It's when you allow yourselves to get out of that place of centeredness and joyfulness that life shows you what you are doing and the accumulation of stuff that you allowed to build up within you. Suddenly there is an explosion. Sometimes in words, and sometimes in anger and frustration. Sometimes things will seem to happen accidentally, but there are no accidents. Something within you has aligned you with what you have attracted.

Remind yourselves you can turn things around and be in the God place. Listen to your favorite music, read a favorite book, or just tune into your inner self. Observe the beauty in nature or the beautiful people in your life. Have gratitude for everything that's going your way. It is in this place of appreciation that you will find that joyfulness can return within moments.

Allow yourselves to go with the flow of your emotions whether they are frustration, anger, fear, doubt, happiness, joy, or fulfillment. Be in that moment. Feel, observe, and allow yourselves to move back into centeredness. You can do it. You have done it, and you know you feel wonderful when you are in that place. Remind yourselves that life does not have to be hard. It does not have to be a struggle. It does not have to be frustrating. It does not have to be full of fear and doubt.

Express yourselves as yourselves and be true to yourself no matter what. That is the most important place to be. Remind yourself on a daily basis that there is no separation between the personality that you identify as yourself and that greater inner soul self that is a part of God. When you came into this earthly existence, you approached life with eagerness and enthusiasm. You wanted to have experiences, different experiences and adventures.

Although we may refer to the inner and outer self, in actuality, there is a blending of it all and no separation. When you block off that inner self you feel weak, powerless, and lonely. Your mind, body, and spirit are always interconnected and always a part of God. Realize that as you move about and have your experiences, there will be times when you will feel separate and cut off. When you feel cut off, it is your emotions telling you to look within, to find that beautiful state of peaceful soothing energy, joy, and well-being. Those authentic feelings will remind you that there is a partnership with All That Is. Somewhere deep in your being, you will remember who you really are and where you came from, that whole, divine, soulful self you are, even when you think you are separate.

Feel this natural state of being. Believe in yourself and that you always have what it takes to live a life of peace, joy, love, and abundance. To live in freedom, fully engaged, without giving your power away to things outside of self. The power is always within. There is nothing that cannot be achieved or experienced when you feel connected to that soulful energy and conscious blending within your God self. As we have said before, there has never been and never will be a separation between this inner and outer self. The feeling of separation is an illusion.

You are free to live the life of your inner voice. The choice is totally up to you. When the personality you know as you, which includes your ego and physical self, is aligned with your inner, broader, expansive God self, you are in the zone. Some who exemplified this conscious partnership are Martin Luther King Jr., Eleanor Roosevelt, Nelson Mandela, and Amantine Lucile Aurore Dupin better known as George Sand, Helen Keller, Leonardo da Vinci, Ludwig von Beethoven, Victoria Woodhull, and the Wright Brothers. All of these people refused to allow outside pressures to deter them from being inner directed and true to the self.

It is our purpose to inspire you to expand your vibratory awareness, discover your inner identity, and merge your personality ego self with that soul self. When you do, you feel exuberant and self-assured. Your intentions are clear, and you expect the best. Your entire world becomes magical. Synchronicities are commonplace. Opportunities find you. Relationships are easy, joy-filled, enriching, fruitful and harmonious. You naturally express unconditional love and acceptance. Negative people or horrific news does not disrupt, disturb, or influence your peacefulness. This synergistic relationship with self and everything outside of self culminates in the visceral knowing that cooperation, safety, health, vitality, infinite abundance, freedom, and well-being are the fundamental facts of life. You benefit from, and feel worthy and deserving of All That Is.

QUESTIONS AND ANSWERS

Ken: Can you talk a little about powerlessness and reclaiming your power when you have let some circumstance or outer event take you out of that God zone?

Orion: Yes. When you allow an event or person to affect your state of being, you have given away a part of yourself. You have allowed the circumstance, individual, or event to come into your conscious awareness, and you then feel depleted, lethargic, and powerless. You often feel like you have no options. So how do you reclaim that which is always there, your power? By realizing that what has occurred, you have created. That the situation has happened as a result of your thoughts and feelings.

We remind you that any given situation or event is just a flash of time and it need not become anchored in your beingness. Everything is temporary. It is when you allow yourself to carry the burden or baggage of unhappiness, fear, doubt, or anger that it can totally deplete you or make you ill. Know that if you can create the muck and the mire, you can also create happiness and joy. Reclaiming your power is just as easy as giving it away. You do not have to carry all this stuff with you or relive the angst-filled moment over and over. You can allow it to slide away.

Linda: Something I have noticed within myself is that I am a sensitive and feeling person and am influenced by other people's negativity easily. For example, someone may say something that makes me feel bad, and even though I may try to intellectually tell myself that they didn't mean it or it doesn't matter what they think, it's hard to find a better feeling thought or think my way out of an unhappy place. Do you have some guidance?

Orion: Yes. First, realize that you are a sensitive person and you know you can allow things to bring you into this place of not liking where you are or what you're feeling. Acknowledge that it is what it is and that you are feeling the emotion of it. Allow yourself to move into and through those feelings. Yes, you are sensitive, but do you need to carry those feelings with you? Do you need to continue in that space? You can embrace it. It's fine. Be true to yourself. If you are feeling the pain and the anger, feel it. However, it does not have to paralyze you from moving forward. Remind yourself you can turn the emotions around to love, joy, and happiness just as quickly as sadness, hurt, and fear. It is a moment. It does not need to linger for days and months.

Ken: Are there times when we stay stuck in the familiar because it is within our comfort zone?

Orion: It is often in the complacency of a situation that you will provide for yourselves something that will inch you out of that place, present other opportunities. Sometimes, however, people need an extra kick in the butt to move themselves out of complacency, inactivity, and stagnation. Your inner self knows your current desires and your potentials according to your belief systems, so it will attract situations that will disrupt that comfort zone.

It is the creation of your thoughts, feelings, and emotions that keeps the momentum of self growing, learning, achieving, being, and expanding.

Linda: I have made the mistake of thinking that when you are on the leading edge, there are not enough people who resonate with the work you do, and you start putting up all of these doubts. If you just do something because you love it, and you're confident and you're excited, people will be attracted to you, right?

Orion: Yes, many doors open when you all allow yourself to live and be that which you want to be. Remind yourself that there are no limitations except those you create.

Linda: When you believe in yourself and you are confident, people do want to hear more. If you talk timidly and are unconsciously thinking that they don't want to hear what you are saying, they will respond accordingly.

Orion: Yes, so just relax. Expect the best to find you without doubt, fear, struggle, or strife.

CHAPTER 15

The Power of Appreciation

The rule is that change is a constant. So if the rule is change, how does one become grateful and compassionate for what they already have? When what they have leaves, moves, or is no longer in existence, how does one adapt? You adapt easily if you are in the flow of life, if you are enjoying what is and if you are living in the moment rather than projecting yourself into the past or the future. You adapt to change by enjoying what you have and being in the mode of gratitude and appreciation for your life, your family, your friends, your acquaintances, and your home. By appreciating and loving your life as you live it from moment to moment. When you see through the eyes of appreciation and gratefulness and you love what is, you have everything you need.

Life is miraculous. Look around and see how every living creature is in perfect harmony. When you reflect upon something that no longer exists your life, perhaps something that has been taken away, or someone you have lost, you feel emptiness or a void. However, by focusing on what is and those things that you do have, and truly living in the moment, you begin to appreciate those things and people even more. You become accustomed, through your thoughts, feelings, and emotions, to having certain things in certain ways in your life. When there is change, you must begin to develop new ways of looking at things, new habits of thought and feeling, a new beginning.

Everything is here on a temporary basis. Everything that is in existence is here for a mere speck of time, so to speak. When you view your life and everything in it through the eyes of love, acceptance, and appreciation, you are living in the moment and enjoying what is. No matter what your life brings you, it is as a result of your thoughts, feelings, and emotions. Therefore, when things change, it is because something has changed within you. Realize that that change is a miraculous event giving you more choices, more events to look at from a new perspective.

Create your life from whatever vantage point you can find, but we would suggest looking at it through the vantage point of appreciation, gratitude, and love. For when you look through those eyes and realize that everything that is in your existence is there because of your creation, you can observe it, feel it, be in it, and know the creator that you are. You can accept that change is part of growth and experience.

Be in appreciation for your life's journey, for that is what is moving you forward toward new directions, new beginnings, and new adventures. When you look through this vantage point, you know that from wherever you are, you can create a brand new adventure. Creation is the root from which your life's experiences begin. Enjoy yourself. Do not fret about seeing change in your life, for that is a part of growth, part of the self you are shedding in order to create something new. Be in appreciation of all that is, and love your life as you continually learn and grow.

As you live in the mode of appreciation, you expand your conscious awareness of yourself. You see the beauty that surrounds you. You accept and love even those people who may have seemingly pushed your buttons. You look within to discover the true nature of your being. Appreciation allows you to grow within yourself and to be more accepting of others and life itself. The cultivation of gratitude will attract to you an abundant and fruitful life.

The attitude of gratitude not only produces more abundance in one's life, but also enhances your feelings of worthiness and self-esteem. The more you ride the inspirational momentum of the art of appreciation, the more you will passionately move forward in your life.

Sometimes being inspired by someone or something outside of yourself will assist in launching forgotten ideas and passions. In this place of appreciation and passion, you will rediscover the power to bring your fervent desires to fruition. Feel the energy available when you express appreciation for all you presently do and have with confidence and expectation. Speak and declare all the great things coming to you. Do not give your power to anyone or anything outside of the self.

QUESTIONS AND ANSWERS

Ken: I think we get paralyzed to act when we attach ourselves to the past or to our fear. We then do not allow new opportunities to come. Is that why you say it's so important to live in the moment?

Orion: Yes. To live in the moment and appreciate what is already in your existence, rather than fearing what might happen. Viewing it from that standpoint of the now moment, you have the power to create, to form, to choose, and to observe all of those things that you have created thus far, and what you want to create next. If you look at what you have already created and do not want as negative, it is difficult to appreciate it. We look at it as positive. As moving forward, on to new adventures. As your enthusiasm for life grows, so the momentum continues. Your enthusiasm creates more enthusiasm for creating what you want. It's constant change, constant movement forward.

Ken: Making peace with what is is definitely better than judging or putting down or being afraid of what is, because that is also paralyzing and immobilizing. In a sense, it seems it can keep us from making any progress, expanding, or evolving. We can stay in situations that make us feel safe, and that is why we may not take the time to figure out what we really want. We are afraid that getting what we want will put us in a situation that's going to require more responsibilities than we feel we can handle.

Orion: Yes, it makes you feel fragile or vulnerable or not good about self. Making a change feels very uncomfortable at first. It feels safer staying where you are. You fear that stepping forward might mean mistakes or failure. It might lead to self-judgment.

Yet, if you look at your life and don't judge yourself, but realize that there are no mistakes made, then your experiences are just something that you will grow from. That where you have been was beneficial in those moments. If you get to the next step and you realize that it feels uncomfortable, it feels a little shaky, remind yourself that change can do that. That you are making the decision for growth from the perfect place of where you are, knowing that where you're going will be perfect as well. There are no missteps. There is only growth experience. No judgments.

Chapter 16

In-Joying Life!

Trusting and Allowing

How do you trust? What are the components of trusting? Trusting is when you, the individual, are self-assured and know that all is well. When you expect the best in everyone and everything. Belief in self and your harmonious relationship with the process of life is the main component of trust. You have the indicators along the way, one being your intuition, which is your inner guidance. Trusting that gut feeling, trusting those impulses and instincts from your non-physical self is a part of the process of being engaged with life. When you tap into that wisdom, feel the brushing of your thoughts, you will feel that the information you are given is something you instinctually know. You will then follow the inner guidance and you will not be lead astray.

As you progress, you become the powerful being that you are, and allow yourself the privilege and pleasure of knowing that what is being given to you at any moment comes from your greater non-physical self. Trust and allow and make decisions according to your inner guidance, even when there may be external conditions provoking fears. Practice discerning, from the wisdom of your inner self, those fears that provoke quick action and push events. Don't go until you know. When you are synergistically aligned with your whole soul self, your decisions will be effortless and your life will synchronistically unfold in fulfillment and joy.

When something seems out of whack, when something feels off kilter, off base, and you can't find your way back to the path, stop and breathe and feel and trust your self to know what the next step for you is. When you cannot find the light, go to this inner space. Bathe in it, bask in it, and see for yourself what has placed you in that state of despair. Reflect on your experiences. Even in fear and despair, you can go within. Think about something or someone that has given you happiness and joy. Remind yourself that by thinking differently you can bring yourself one-step closer to the light. That you can turn despair and disharmony into hopefulness.

You have a soul-ution to any challenge when you trust and allow the inner information to flow through you as you. You will understand more fully than ever before in your life when you trust your instincts and allow them to be a part of you. By tuning in, listening, paying attention, discerning for yourself, and not allowing anything else to dissuade you from your instinctual knowing, you will be guided every day along your pathway. It will become a natural part of your life experience, bringing you closer to what you desire.

Enjoy the process as you live a more natural life with ease, without resistance, without being hard on yourselves. Do not allow outer circumstances to dictate your inner well-being. Do not allow what is going on around you to punch a hole in that beautiful space you call your life, your beingness.

When you allow yourselves to trust and be and to believe what you have discerned for yourself, you are always aware of the guidance along the way. You know what is best for you. Trust and allow your vibrational casting studio with your casting manager and all your agents to bring you the synchronizations of the process of life—health, material things, harmonious relationships, everything and anything that you have fantasized about.

Life is you enjoying from the inside out. Life is your friend, your beingness, your joyfulness, your frustrations, your sorrows, your feelings of powerlessness. It is also everything you see, feel, and touch. Be inspired by that which is called your life, the wholeness of you—mind, body, and spirit. You are here to enjoy the magnificent dance. You are not only meant to be the witness and observer, but also the participant.

It is indeed a joy for us when we see you engaged in the dance of life. Be in the here and now. Enjoy from the inside out. Your inner guidance will show you what will be reflected in the outward beingness of your dreams, desires, and wishes. Bask in life as it drenches you all with love, light, beauty, and wonderment. Know that you are all intuitive beings, and by listening to your intuition, you can be guided by that which you know to be true. Have fun with life. Dance with All That Is. It is the process of life that affords you experiential knowing.

Once your ego—your physically focused self—reawakens to the recognition of your alignment with your inner self, you will restructure and rewire your entire neurological being. Your new emotional responses will be more positive and life affirming. Your vibration frequency will be enhanced. Consequently, you will start to see miraculous new synchronicities, opportunities, experiences, and events appear almost effortlessly in your lives.

Believe and trust and know that what's being received by you is from your Godself, your God Zone, your powerful point of existence. In that powerful point of existence when you reflect upon the word empower, replace the E with I.The *I* of you. *I* am power. Enjoy, *in*-joy, *inner* joy. I am joy. Inspire, *in*-spirit. I am spirit. In reflecting upon such words, allow the feeling and inner knowing to rush over you. Feel the God of you. The worthiness, the abundance, the love, the creative power of you.

Be one with self. Be true to that self. Feel the ease of the you that you are, the comfort of that feeling.

Proclaim, "I am God, a part of All That Is." Be it, feel it, know it, live it from the inside out.

Ken: So how would you define the process and life?

Orion: Life is a magical mystery tour.

Ken: I love that.

~ The End ~

ABOUT THE AUTHOR

Photo: Vickie Rogers

Leslie Stewart has studied metapsychics for over 30 years from both physical and nonphysical teachers, and assisted her life-partner Ken Routson—author, workshop presenter, life coach, and management consultant—in conducting workshops nationwide for 25 years. She is inspired by Louise Hay, Wayne Dyer, Jane Roberts and Seth, and influenced by her interactions with spirit teachers Abraham, Amel and Teach. Leslie has worked and studied in the medical field, including *Body Talk*.

Years ago before she started to channel, she was aware of her healing abilities when she would discover herself ouside of her body at night visiting those who requested her assistance in healing. She proceeded her channeling with automatic writing and after six months she started to channel Orion. Leslie is president of Tulip Press Publishing Co. She has been involved with Individual Growth & Fulfillment, a seminar and consulting company for 22 years.

CPSIA information can be obtained
at www.ICGtesting.com
Printed in the USA
BVOW06s0821110917
494530BV00014B/219/P